CAPITALS

A POETRY ANTHOLOGY

CAPITALS

A POETRY ANTHOLOGY

Edited by

ABHAY K.

B L O O M S B U R Y

NEW DELHI • LONDON • OXFORD • NEW YORK • SYDNEY

First published, 2016

BLOOMSBURY PUBLISHING INDIA PVT. LTD.
New Delhi London Oxford New York Sydney

ISBN: 978-93-86141-11-8

10 9 8 7 6 5 4 3 2 1

Published by Bloomsbury Publishing India Pvt. Ltd.
DDA Complex LSC, Building No. 4, 2nd Floor
Pocket 6 & 7, Sector C
Vasant Kunj, New Delhi 110070

Cover Image: Holy Geographic Elephant by Tarshito |2011 / 2014| mixed media: acrylic, gold leaf and khanta stitch on canvas, cm 200 x 140 (h)

Printed and bound in India by Replika Press Pvt Ltd

This anthology is dedicated to
the call for an official Earth Anthem

CONTENTS

INTRODUCTION

'I have never felt salvation in nature. I love cities above all.'
—Michelangelo

Capitals are considered the highest achievement of human civilization in terms of art, literature and architecture. Countries are sometimes addressed by their capitals. India is referred to as New Delhi, Russia as Moscow, and the United States as Washington DC. Generally each country has one national capital; however there are a few countries which have more than one capital. For example South Africa has three capitals while Bolivia has two. Some countries such as Monaco or Vatican are synonymous with their capitals. Other countries do not have a capital at all, for example, Nauru does not have a capital city. Certain cities are also known as world capitals, for example, London and New York often compete for the title of the world capital.

The word *Capital* is derived from Latin *Capitalis* meaning 'of the head,' hence 'capital, chief, first'. Capitals are seats of political and often financial power and thus provide patronage to the finest art and culture including poetry. No wonder, architect Daniel Libeskind says—'Cities are the greatest creations of humanity.'

Our planet is divided into more than 193 sovereign nation-states, each with their own power-centers located in their capital cities. In contemporary times, the flow of ideas, people and goods among these capitals is greater than smaller cities or towns. Thus, capitals are at the forefront of making a truly cosmopolitan global society.

After travelling to many countries and to their capitals as a poet and as a diplomat I feel that capitals are tied together by a common thread despite their seeming differences on the surface. As Italo Calvino, the author of *The Invisible Cities* has put it so succinctly—'Travelling, you realize that differences are lost: each city takes to resembling all cities, places exchange their form, order, distances, a shapeless dust cloud invades the continents.'

Each day a legion of diplomats, parliamentarians and officials travel to these capitals to carry out the affairs of the state. Businessmen, tourists, students, journalists and workers travel for commerce, sightseeing, visiting friends and relatives, education, reporting and employment. A large number of travel writers and photographers visit all corners of our planet and publish their travelogues and photographs. They are all consciously or unconsciously helping the world to come together, creating a close-knit community of global citizens aware of the exquisite beauty and diversity of our planet.

Cities have always fascinated me. I grew up in Nalanda, Bihar before moving to New Delhi for higher studies. I studied Geography at the Kirorimal College, Delhi University and later at the Jawaharlal Nehru University. After joining the Indian Foreign Service, I worked in New Delhi, Moscow, St. Petersburg and Kathmandu before moving to Brasilia. As part of my work, I often visit the capitals of different countries at very short notice. I look for poems on places I visit before setting out as I believe poems have the ability to render a deep and intimate experience of a place.

As a frequent traveler I often felt the need of a poetry atlas but I could not find one. So I decided to create one. I set out on an impossible journey of finding a poem on each capital city of the world. These lines from the play 'Hassan' by James Elroy Flecker, one of many distinguished world poets who worked for the consular service, inspired me—'Caliph Haroun Al Raschid—Ah, if there shall ever arise a nation whose people have forgotten poetry or whose poets have forgotten the people, though they send their ships round Taprobane and their armies across the hills of Hindustan, though their city be greater than Babylon of old, though they mine a league into earth or mount to the stars on wings—what of them? Hassan—They will be a dark patch upon the world.'

I wanted to light my own candle in the darkness. The journey looked arduous. I did not know many poets outside my own country. I asked for help from those whom I knew, thinking they would know poets from every country. I was surprised to find out

that even the most well-connected poets, in their sixties, did not know poets from two-thirds of the world. I was at loss. A poetry anthology on the capital cities looked impossible. Unfazed, I kept trying. The hope of meeting poets whom I had never known, reading their poems and possibly meeting them someday gave me strength. The internet provided me means to connect with them.

Poetry Parnassus curated by Simon Armitage alongside the London Olympics in 2012 came as the only close parallel to this ambitious anthology. An anthology titled *World Record* was published on the occasion containing works of the poets who participated in the Parnassus. A BBC report of that time informs us that the organizers of the Poetry Parnassus in London had difficulties in finding poets from Monaco and a host of other countries. A public call went to twenty-three countries to send their poets to represent them in the Poetry Parnassus. I also could not find poems on a number of capitals despite my best efforts.

I learned that poets from Europe and America were well connected to each other compared to the poets from Africa and Asia. I faced difficulties in finding poets from countries where Arabic, Spanish, French and Portuguese are spoken. It was difficult to find a good translator who could translate their works into English.

As J.D. McClatchy quotes Aristotle in *The Vintage Book of Contemporary World Poetry*—'The basis of all poetry is metaphor. Nothing can be freshly or truly seen in itself until it is seen first as something else. It is this image-making impulse that unifies world poetry, and gives it its spiritual force.' This anthology tries to bring out the distinct images and individual experiences of the capital cities through poetry.

It is a unique anthology that covers most of the planet. It brings together poets of different genres and ages. Most have written about their own capital cities, giving a great degree of intimateness and individuality to their poems. However, there are a few poets who have contributed poems on the cities travelled and explored by them. So there is also the outsider's perspective on some cities. I ask your graceful indulgence for the poems I have penned

and added to the anthology. These cities were not represented, and I was drawn to write on those I know.

The anthology is ordered alphabetically—Africa, Americas, Asia-Pacific and Europe. I have merged North, Central and South America into one region—the Americas, and brought a few countries of Oceania into Asia-Pacific because of their geographical proximity.

The anthology begins with a poem on Abuja, the new capital of Nigeria, by Jumoke Verissimo—'Signpost/This capital is under construction/So enter into this rock town/shaped like a mug/ and see that/still when nothing happens/it moves into the news.' She adds further—'I watch you – struggle to become/a city with a soul./On the shoulder of trembling grounds/your eyes though open cannot see/the earth is shifting. You're saving sand./I will not be swallowed. I'll move on.' The poet takes us to Abuja's dark underworld and bares her soul. She expresses her deep fears of being swallowed and at the same time hopes to move on.

Kwame Dawes in his poem *Green Boy* takes us to a night in Accra when drums are heard instead of the sound of guns—'That night, they stared into/the orange dusk over Accra, poured libation,/ listening for guns first, but soon/it was drums, the celebration.'

Liyou Libsekal describes Addis Ababa—'this dappled green core pulses with early song/taxi boys in convulsive refrain.' In Christopher Merrill's Algiers—'the ash fall hasn't reached the city, and yet the sky at noon is pitch-black.' Betsy Orlando visualizes Antananarivo as a lady walking with grace carrying a basket on her head. In Bamako, a lady longs for a husband. Grandmaster Masese proclaims the immortality of the capital of the Central African Republic—'Bangui never dies.'

I had heard a lot from my diplomat friends about Cape Town, one of the three capitals of South Africa, but had never imagined Gabeba Baderoon's visualization of Cape Town in her poem—'I step on the old silences of the city./What can explain/this exact and unjust beauty?/In the last flash of the sun, the city gleams/ white and hard as bone.'

I have never been to Conakry but Gerard Noiret's poem on Conakry instantly makes me feel the heat of this capital city in

capital letters—'WHO FORGOT TO INVENT SHADE IN THIS COUNTRY?'

Charlotte Hill O'Neal reminisces about her city 'In Memories of Dar es Salaam,'—'Charcoal smell wraps 'round *makaa* coals/ Sizzling and fizzling and assaulting my nostrils/with acrid sweet odors that I will never forget.'

Tim Cummings finds old men squatting in the heat of the sun in Khartoum—'Time moves like grain through wood,/memory opening up like a palm,/fermenting in buckets for moonshine/ booze that scrambles the eyes/of old men squatting in the heat/of the sun, generous in its embrace.'

Sita Namwalie's Kigali—'... is a mirror of shifting moods,/A place of heaving seasons.'

Frank M. Chipasula brings out the racial and linguistic fissures in Lilongwe evocatively in his poem—'Though the white city curses the black/in fluent Afrikaans, it stutters on the bird-/lime of Mandarin and carefully broken English.'

Meg Pierce finds herself yawning in Lome where—'The din of night,/meanders into early morn./Under the motionless,/moonlit sky a lone moto/hums along, silently scattering/plastic scraps./I yawn.'

Jekwu Ozoemene is stared down by an angry sun in Lusaka. Yusuf Adamu's Niamey is a capital of contrasts and segregation. Only a poet can compare the river Niger to a mirror in which Niamey refuses to see its face—'In this city of contrasts, the city of segregation/I breathe the scent of Hausaland in Zango/In this brownish city of lower and upper markets/I see the new capital refusing to see its face/In the mirror of the river Niger.'

Karla Brundage can't forget Yamoussoukro of her mother's days and with great pain writes—'The wildlife is gone/No ivory left in the Ivory Coast/It is cliché to tell young people that/The elephants have gone/My students don't care/They want an iphone 6.'

Joseph Brodsky remarked once—'What I like about cities is that everything is king size, the beauty and the ugliness.' Viola Allo's Yaounde is a such a mish-mash of contrasts—'I see the

maddening mish-mash/of wealth and adversity, and/I squeeze my father's hand,/clamber back into his car and stay there.'

Poems on African capitals take us on a journey through memories, sounds of silence, drums, birds, taxis and guns; racial tensions, segregation, heat, natural beauty, loss of wildlife and a growing craze for modern gadgets. We see Africa in all its vibrant colours through these poems.

Our poetic journey of the Americas begins with a poem by Imruh Bakri on Basseterre, the capital of the Federation of St. Kitts and Nevis, the smallest sovereign state in Americas in area and population. In his poem he writes—'The circus clock/was standing still/and going nowhere/when Marcus Garvey/stood on Basseterre Bay Road/not far from the old slave/market in Pall Mall Square/His voice took the sea/breeze inland/where volcanic rock resides.'

Amparo Osorio's Bogota is—'like a swarm of fallen angels/the afternoon's reddish clouds descend/In the hollow of the city' and 'it is impossible /to meditate in silence.' Marcus Freitas's Brasilia is a—'city without traditions' living in 'half a century of solitude/ within the central highlands.'

Linda M. Deane writes about Bridgetown—'we kill more Time—/another round and later, leave the way we came,/passing men and boys at ground level, still/*Playing games at the edge of Bridgetown.'*

Buenos Aires is—'an invisible city, continuing, made of messages/Strung together by those who have most cherished/ The lucid pleasures of thought,' in words of Clive Wilmer. In Marcela Sulak's Caracas—'it´s raining/on her bright breasts, it´s raining on her belly/down her thighs; the people below are wet/ with stolen light.'

Mark Mcwatt's has many Georgetowns in his memory fleeing—'Georgetowns of my memory flee/from me now, taking with them/those long-lost houses, whose quiet corners/and dark, hiding cupboards used to sing/songs of comfort and belonging.'

Pedro Pérez Sarduy in his poem *Searching for an Unemployed Lover* writes—'Havana lives on the edge of darkness/with its air contaminated by tourists/and uncommon dissidents./Havana was

there mine and more sensual than usual/leaning out as always from her balconies.'

'On Kingston's flat worn earth,/everything is hard as glass./The sun smashes into the city—no breath,/no wind, just the engulfing, asthmatic noonday'—writes Kwame Dawes about the capital of Jamaica.

In the evening in Ernesto Cardenal's Managua—' the neon lights are soft/and the mercury streetlamps, pale and beautiful/And the red star on a radio tower/in the twilight sky of Managua/looks as pretty as Venus.' *Zoe Brigley's M*exico City—'is an island like a jewel or scarab/on the flat lagoon where herons wade./They walk the circling zócalo from city door/to city gate.'

Luis Bravo's Montevideo—'is not a city for tourists but for explorers of the spirit, in Montevideo the poets dream a dream within a dream.'

In Alfred Corn's New York—'They stare back into an increate future,/Dead stars, burning still.' Lucy Cristina Chau's Panama City is surreal—'while you're sleeping—/a woman is drawing herself/using the precise lines of the infinite/and preparing—as in an invented ritual—/the clandestine meeting/with your kisses.'

In Derek Walcott's Port of Spain—'Night, the black summer, simplifies her smells/into a village; she assumes the impenetrable/musk of the negro.' Delroy Nesta Williams asks—'How do you walk through Roseau/And not smell the stench?'

Luis Chaves's—'San Jose was nothing but/some lights in the distance:/a bureaucratic constellation/looking a little less underdeveloped in the dark.' In Veronica Zondek's Santiago—'Pregnancy is a circumstance./LIfe is weird/and stretches out as a statistic./Death hides away behind thick walls/in a black disposable bag.' Jael Uribe's Santo Domingo is a place where—'Happy people/run wild in the streets/shadows dance on concrete.' Alex Bramwell finds the Bolivian capital confounding—'The city of the House of Freedom/has four names and forty languages/but all words are the same.'

In Kim Roberts' Washington DC—'The Lincoln sinks into the Potomac/with a sigh' while in Myra Skalrew's Washington DC earth talks—'In this freest city. Oh if earth/could talk. Earth does

talk in the neatly framed yards/where death thinks to lay us down to rest. Asleep,/the marker stones.'

Journey to each capital seems a journey to the wonderland, as if riding on a broomstick, flying around the world. Could there be a better way to see Asia than through the eyes of the poets and to begin with Ankara, the capital of Turkey?

Look at Müesser Yeniay's Ankara fending for itself alone like a widow—'cold, winters, leaves piercing/inside the body of a girl/—Ankara is alone like a widow' or Astana of Temirkhan Medetbek for that matter—'It is so bitter cold here/that your spittle becomes ice/and face swells/as a pumpkin.'

Poet Salah Al Hamdani's Baghdad is a fallen city—'Oh Baghdad/cursed city/like you perhaps, I'll die among exiles/and I'll bind my tears to yours/and to those of your impotent gods.' In Arthur Sze's Beijing—'man hauling coal in the street is stilled forever./Inside a temple, instead of light/a slow shutter lets the darkness in.'

Poet P.S. Cottier's Canberra is a city 'built as a compromise.' Michelle Cahill finds Canberra with—'A swathe of poppies, memorial to Darafshan,/a father's odium for the rogue soldier.'

Two poems on Jerusalem, one by Asa Boxer, another by Mahmoud Darwish, show us different visions of the historic city. Asa Boxer brings out terror hiding in nooks and crannies of the city in his poem—'Terror lives in the cornerstones, and in the small/monuments around what seems like every bend./Terror at the children murdered in their dawdling.' Mahmoud Darwish's poem translated by Fady Joudah has altogether a different vision and depth—'In Jerusalem, and I mean within the ancient walls,/I walk from one epoch to another without a memory/to guide me. The prophets over there are sharing/the history of the holy.'

Ali Al Jallawi's Manama sheds tears—'Like two sycamores/Like doves/Landing on a wire of his ideas/God poured from his chest/His knees dropped onto a star/And nearby, Manama cried.' Marra PL. Lanot's Manila is—'... rich with the warm/Spit of barbers and shoeshine boys,/Of guitars strumming for stolen chickens/Manila that is mother earth/For it is brave enough to own/Heroes killed for unremembered cause.'

Ashjan Hendi ruminates on Riyadh—'Let my dreams reach the sky/please don't wake me up/and don't ask me why/dreams should be sweet/when they come true/in luscious Riyadh.' Kim Gyeongmee advises on how to eat in Seoul—'Be a heart like the bean sprouts boiled to the core/Never spill a single grain of the quiet in the shade of rice.' Alvin Pang tells us—'if S'pore exists, if it is to be/found within the bounds/of this island and not just/in the colour of my passport, of my smart card.'

Sudesh Mishra's Suva is a happy place—'Yes, it rings true: we are the happy few./We have been kept in the dark for so long/ We see in it the first stirrings of dawn.' Hamid Ismailov reflects on his life in Tashkent—'In your life you'll still write another/twenty five books in the little square/among the mass of stone, ugly memorials.'

'I love to travel in the night in dark streets of Tbilisi'—writes Sabrina Masud and then explores the city's history, myths and legends through her poem. In her poem on Tehran Mimi Khalvati asks—'What if the city/that gave credence to your sickness/were as vanished as the home/you took for granted you would bless/ with success and happy children?'

In Jan Napier's Tokyo—'... nights are charred paper./Whispers transform them to flakes of ash/the wind lifts and whirls like fairy skirts.' G. Mend-Ooyo writes about the sparrows of Ulaan Baatar—'The last leaves tear from the trees and fly away./A flock of sparrows come in to take their place.'

Bryan Thao Worra Vientiane is a—'Sandalwood city/The moon hangs high above us/Night fragrant and calm./So many temples here,/Monuments and kind people/The Buddha strolls by.' In Jennifer Compton's Wellington—'There is a darkness..: and also an itinerant rainbow/strolling like a twister with one lazy finger dipped in water.' Lola Koundakjian sees in her dreams in Yerevan nights—'herself on a bed of clouds/Reclining/Reposing.'

Europe is presented in different moods from Helsinki to Nicosia, from Dublin to Moscow by European poets and those from other places.

Joris Lenstra writes about Amsterdam—'He's got a mouth like a river, juicy and toothless./Everybody loves him because he's

willing to shoulder anything/Without ever complaining./He shifts tons through small waterways to Germany.' In Andorra la Vella of Ester Fenoll Garcia—'the sky and lakes/guard the silence of dawn.'

In Athens it is so hot that Claire Askew is at loss—'All night, under the chattering fans,/I think about the girl's chapped throat,/ the boy she lies beside,/their mouths. None of us sleeps.' She adds—'Things that thrive here: mules/and stones, crickets loud as fire alarms,/the harder vines. Old women/whose hands and feet are tough,/whose men worked boats or built homes/all day in the big heat,/and died young.'

In Jelena Lengold's Belgrade—'The old people in…street/walk in the park every day staking their life with their cane/like leaves./ Sometimes they stake through the heart of a young green leaf/ which utters a moan.' Milan Dobricic's Belgrade carries—'The smell of linden-trees/a tremor of water/the scuttling of sparrow.'

Hatto Fischer is in a state of shock in Berlin—'That was not what I had expected to see, Berlin at the end of the bar, mind you the Einstein café was created by an architect friend from Hamburg, and who went to Paris for the materials to cover the seats and sofas, while the carpenter of this longest bar had already fitted out Onassis' yacht.'

Brigitte Fuchs compares Bern with a bear after which the city is named—'Since he lent the city its name, he holds/the Berner (clumsy and unhurried) on his toes.' Charles Baudelaire lands up in Willem Roggeman's Brussels—'with a burning suitcase full of melancholy/…in order to escape his creditors/and in the hope of finding a publisher/for all of his poems.'

In Astrid Alben's Bucharest—'Distant voices hum along arthritic electricity poles./Ravens lick their scabs.' George Szirtes's Budapest—'… offers you no evidence/Except the collage of the overheard,/Extended clauses of a broken sentence.'

Phillip Nikolayev reminisces about his happy Soviet childhood days in Moldova's capital—'Those were days of cholera epidemics/in Moldova. We'd buy peasant-cooked/fodder corn on the cob when we got hungry,/haggled with old ladies over pennies.'

Philip McDonagh writes about Copenhagen—'At Horsholm, Holte, and along the coast/the subfusc autumn colours of the trees;/by every bus-stop workers at their post/before the dawn, in silent companies.'

In Anni Sumari's Helsinki—'snow falls in slow motion/someone wades into the dark/the unpronounced polar dawn is/quelled by snow sweepers.' Anatoly Kudryavitsky's Kiev is—'a gaping wound in the sky./The city has been running/a high fever: buildings swollen,/all the corners rounded.' Xavier Frias Conde's—'Lisbon/ wanders barefoot.' In Les Wicks' London—'Long-distance buses are a sort of death/every bodily function closes down in an odoriferous, slumped shuffle.'

Valzhyna Mort asks in Minsk—'How hard it is to pull ourselves up/from the pose of a question mark/into the pose of an exclamation?' In Phillip Nikolayev's Moscow—'The parks begin to yawn, where statues still/stand half-emphatically, as if leaning/ toward the vacuum of a lost empire.'

'Inconsolable, I gave myself to the sullen/glory of great poems and ended up here, on the/windiest corner of the windy city.' 'Go to Oslo,'/said the young woman, 'there is no wind in Oslo.'—writes Mark Strand.

Remembering her father's city, Pascale Petit writes—'All of Paris is quiet, while the oxygen machine/struggles to fill your lungs.' 'I was wanted in Paris. Paris, astounded by my splendor/ and charmed by my excitable manner,/waited to open its arms to me.'—writes Vijay Seshadri.

Adam Borzic's Prague—'... is dressed up as a warder/In long flowing cloak, the color of rain/Seeks all fragile souls/And every time gives them the same frozen kiss.' Luca Benassi's—'Rome is red sunsets/and golden days swept away from hills/with nothing left/but ruins that nurture a romance.' In Anatoly Kudryavitsky's Sarajevo—'a boy wearing headphones/walks off the edge/into his silent music.' In Sudeep Sen's Sarajevo—'air is memory, memory photo-plates,/plates repository of translucent images/of fire, birth, and now—your time now.'

Magdalena Horvat's—'Skopje is cigarette smoke/its sky pierced by chimneys and factory towers/the language stuck in

our throats, in our lungs.' Kapka Kassabova's Sofia—'is the place where in dark, empty apartments the people you love live inside mirrors.'

Mathura (aka Margus Lattik) remembers Stockholm of his childhood and very poignantly writes—'Stockholm is beautiful. I am ordinary.' In Hasso Krull's Tallinn—'The trees look medieval. A half-naked girl in golden shoes steps out on the street from a cellar. Somebody stops you: hey, do you have a lighter?'

Mathias Ospelt on Vaduz roundabout does not know what to do next—'Should I go now to the 'Löwen'?/Or should I go now to 'Left'?/Should I go to the movies?/Or should I go home to bed/I could also just idle in this roundabout/Staying here wouldn't be so bad/Outside it's way too dangerous/Out there the world's gone mad.'

It is not all rosy in Immanuel Mifsud's Valetta—'A dog's turd in the middle of the street, crowned by a legion of flies. A couple of filthy strays wagging their tail.' Irish poet Pat Boran writes about the Vatican City—'Barbarians inside the gate, we could tear down/ this whole splendid city, this gilded confection, this stunning/insult to the poor, the queer, the fallen out of grace.'

Priya Sarukkai Chabria's Vienna is—'A peephole, an iris closing on itself:/My view of Vienna or von Stroheim's shimmering/film of him playing his dream: the Count immaculate in debauchery.'

This anthology ends with a poem on Zagreb, the capital of Croatia by Tomica Bajsic who waits at an ATM to get hold of a banknote of a thousand Kunas with a portrait of Ante Starčević, the father of Croatia. He ends up complaining that he has grown old waiting in queue to meet the father of his nation.

I learned things from these poems about the capitals of our planet, that I could not learn reading travel guides. The beauty of language, images, metaphors used to describe the capitals is extraordinary. These poems are original expressions of poets inviting us to see our capital cities through their eyes.

Editing this anthology took me over two years. Scottish Poetry Library, Australian Poetry and Theatre without Borders helped me in this endeavour by spreading the word. I faced inherent challenges involved in undertaking such a daunting task; foremost

of these was overcoming the language barrier. Poets who write in Spanish, Portuguese, French, Dutch and Arabic found it difficult to contribute. As a result I have not been able to cover every capital city. I could not get fine poems on some capitals despite my best efforts. I received many poems which were not quite worthy for this anthology and hence rejected them.

The anthology is ready now, and I remember these words of Tony Robbins—'The only impossible journey is the one you never begin.' It has been a tremendous experience to get to know poets from more than 160 countries, to read their poems and see the world in a refreshing way through their words.

Sadly, Mark Strand left us before the completion of this anthology. When I wrote to him requesting contribution on Oslo, he replied instantly in October 2014 with his words—'Go right ahead'. He left us in November 2014. Inara Cedrins who contributed her poems on Beijing and Cairo to this anthology also left us before its completion.

I would like to end with these words of Antoine de Saint-Exupery—'In this century, as in others, our highest accomplishments still have the single aim of bringing people together.' I hope this anthology will enrich us by bridging the communication gap, by connecting the poets of Africa, Asia-Pacific, Americas and Europe. I hope it will intensify creative exchanges leading to the birth of a true global community of poets and poetry lovers.

It is our interconnectedness that enriches us.

—ABHAY K.

AFRICA

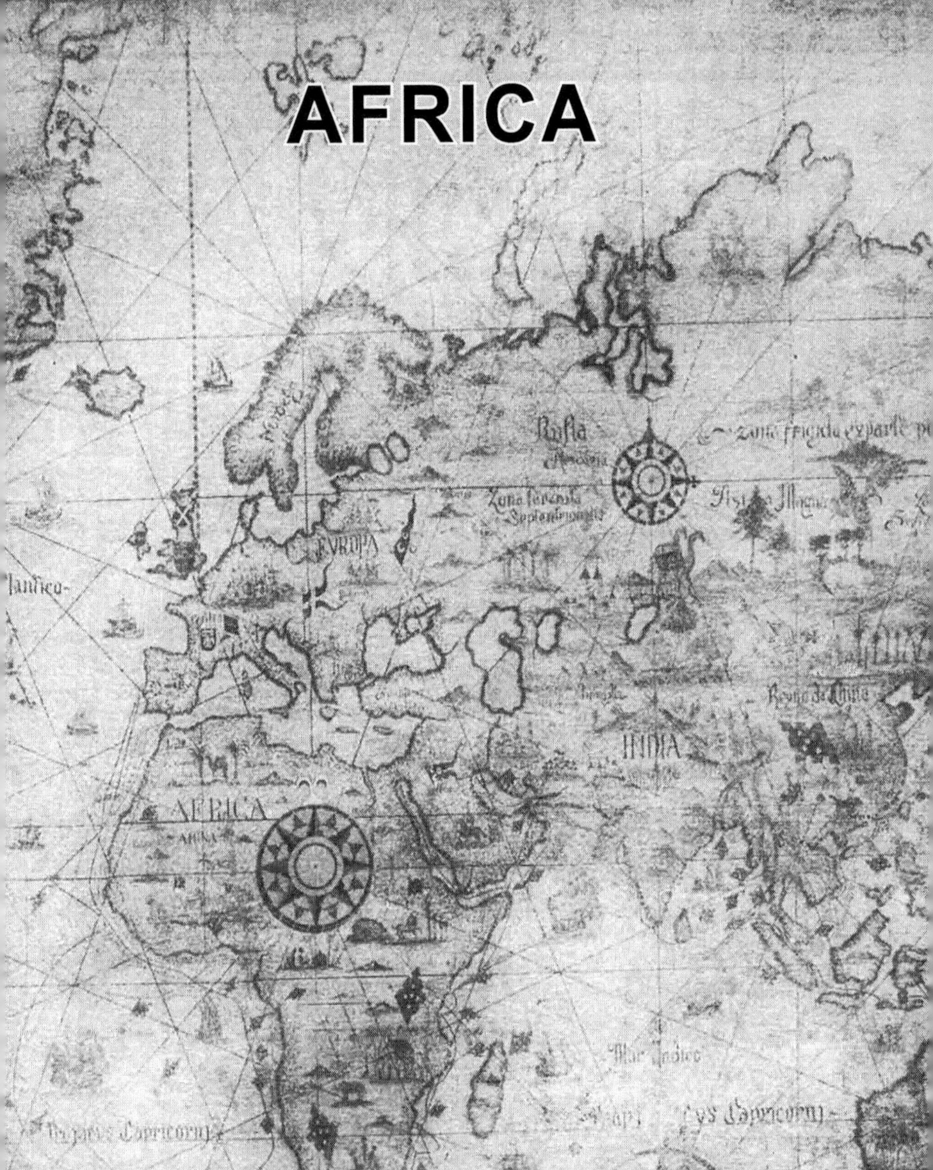

ABUJA

Poems for Abuja

By Jumoke Verissimo

I

Signpost:
This capital is under construction.

So enter into this rock town
shaped like a mug
and see that
still when nothing happens
it moves into the news.

Light against dark ends
poor outside the rich inside
folks move around contrasting
the architecture
with the ties with the land

II

This city is known for its rock
power rock and all those shit.
I watch. Like the world I watch.
power house without power
I watch you – struggle to become
a city with a soul.

On the shoulder of trembling grounds
your eyes though open cannot see
the earth is shifting. You're saving sand.
I will not be swallowed. I'll move on.

III
Signpost: This capital has missing things

Like people, money, lives and hope
This is the centre of the country
North, South, West and East
Our soul moved into their purses
They ate our eyes
Swallowed our voices
But I heard that when
The rock took our voices
We spoke against the ash
Formed from our sweat
With signs like: # # # # #
Wemovedaboutontwitter
Facetofacewebookedourhorror

The world listened.

IV
Barren land with blooming flowers
Is this how you will continue
To
Take from others?

This is a second choice.
Capital non—

ACCRA

Green Boy

By Kwame Dawes

They were looking for a reason
to get drunk, with fists
full of groundnuts and fingers
sweet and slick with oil from
the kelewele; and the news
came that Nkrumah survived
and so did I, wailing,
in Korle bu, there at the center
of a city gleaming with the hope
of revolution—slick, capable
of wiping away blood spilled;
the sweet spot when heroes
were still heroes, and young men
believed in the language of change.

The convenience of a ready
party around me has not
become my fate, though
I have always felt that
some more auspicious
happening has always
cramped my style making
me wait for the party,
me walking through thinking
that maybe I should not
be there, my cheeks hurting
from smiling so hard.

Not that my father did
not love me; he must have

even then, and the toasts were
for me; the one who you
could call the safety net,
in case the first born son,
somehow failed—and anyway,
we Africans know how
perilous the journey to
a woman's vagina can be—
how the soul can linger
deep in the comforting
waters of her pure dark
insides, reluctant to face
the glare of daylight, the stench
of humans, the complications.

Yes, they cheered, for me,
the bonus, the brawta,
the extra, the just-in-case.
We fulfill our births:
I told them I was green;
the room was crowded
when I came—heroes
surviving assassinations,
writers composing epics,
so I wanted to be green
so they could see.

That night, they stared into
the orange dusk over Accra, poured libation,
listening for guns first, but soon
it was drums, the celebration
of the king's survival,
and somewhere in there,
there is this bauble of delight
in a child born, intact, facing decades,
facing decades to come.

ADDIS ABABA

Addis Ab'a

By Liyou Libsekal

this dappled green core pulses with early song, surges
with the bloom of eighty tongues weaving the waking
ensemble of kinetic hills conducting a rhapsodic ruckus

taxi boys in convulsive refrain above murmuring huddles
neighbours' volleyed teases swirling with the ditty of
teenaged virtuosos in coy flirtation, morning mirth
chiming with the coffee woman's clinking steps

the swelling current wafts like a third brew, zinging
a pleasant kind of bitter, an eruption of choral metal and
concrete treading beneath the spiced pep of the khat house boys,
the baby faced rovers, the suited and the coarse-handed
warriors in a precarious dance

scuffling and skidding in a writhing, technicolored din
kicking up dust on streets where dawn's rivers of praise
converged to be swallowed in this elegant clamor

ALGIERS

Algiers

By Christopher Merrill

The ash fall hasn't reached the city, and yet the sky at noon is pitch-black. Children in the Casbah huddle on the steps, shopkeepers pull down their shutters, and a visiting pensioner from the defeated army scans the crowd outside the cinema for the daughter of the man he *persuaded* to reveal the hiding place of his best friend. As the water rises in the harbor, a geography teacher sets his basket down and picks through the garbage heaped below the sea wall, wishing he had obeyed his father's order to study medicine. A fisherman, weighing anchor, studies the couples strolling on the beach, under the reproachful gaze of the young man on the boardwalk who reads too much. Everything—everything!—fires his nerves. The pensioner marches toward the quay, sidestepping a colony of feral cats, which have their eyes on something. *Black and white*, he thinks. *It was all in black and white*. What do the cats see? A dead rat.

ANTANANARIVO

Antananarivo

By Elizabeth Orlando

On her head
A basket
Woven of reed
Filled with bread.

Around her shoulders
A blanket
Slung
In which a baby
Hung.

Her feet
Wore no shoes or lace.
Yet, she walked
With grace.

Her head
Held high
To balance the load
Too busy to ponder
Why
She carried it.

This was her life
This was her load:
A baby, a basket
Did not constitute much strife.
They were better than hunger
And a death's casket.

Feet unshorn
In time inures
All the earth's born.

To the one who really looks
She possesses wealth
In pride and good health.
Two sources of joy
She wears close –
Life-giving bread
And a baby boy.

ASMARA

Her Picture

By Ressom Haile

I wrote to Photo Studio
In The Hague,

Dear Photographer:

Make a portrait
Of my Eritrea –
An African,

But she won't blacken your lens.
Fresh skin
Full blooded and brown,

She glistens.
Her teeth and wide eyes
Gleam.

I want her head to toe,
The whole body,
Not one of your Mona Lisas.

Forget the Venus de Milo.
Reveal the beauty
Of her hands

And her figure
As she stands,
Crushes a snake
With her heel
Like Mother Mary
And looks at me.

Also show how colors flash
From her dress
With her shawl, kerchief and sash.

Patience, Photo Lucas.
Patience, Foto Zula.
She's in Europe now,

But someday in Asmara,
Ambling on Liberation Avenue,
She'll come to you
For her picture.

—*Translated by* Charles Cantalupo

BAMAKO

Bamako

By Karla Brundage

For CK

On the River Niger—brown and murky
We eat dinner with silver spoons
As women wash clothes in the evening shade
that Touareg blue against the brown earth—
resembling the sky

At night, we argue about whether
Africa is indeed home
for African American people

I do not even speak any language,
not French, not Arabic, not Bambara
She has mastered them all

An aunt hennas my hands—a symbol of marriage
As I cry inconsolably over my latest break up
American men—so troubled in their heads
and hearts—are unable to commit

I receive a rock and a blessing
something to keep
promising a good marriage
ten years have passed, I am still single

In her house she has a biche
We are surrounded by walls of a castle
and out there is a man
who waters an entire field

of maize with a bucket
he pulls from a well

I watch him pull
the tiny bucket up
time and again
and then walk down the row
to nourish the plants

I keep wishing he had a pump and a hose
I keep wishing I had a husband.

BANGUI

Bangui

By Grand Master Masese

Bangui,
Who could remember to smile
when those guns fed us lead
In Bangui our hearts bled
Crying for sanity
Bangui,
Who remembers Stanley's fatal whip on our backs
Chopped arms, now firearms in Bangui
Lighting Ubangi with flowing dead blood
Bangui never dies
Determined to silence the ghosts of Brazza
Leopold, Bozize and Bokassa
I stand bold with African pride
I have died many times before
Made to kiss the aroma of mother Congo
And still I germinate
Bangui, I am a seed
I will never die
I will never wither
I will gyrate with the rhythms of Cavacha, Rhumba and Samba
Let the dust of the boots drown in Ubangi
Bangui.

BANJUL

The City By The Atlantic

By Mariama Khan

Once a jewel of the Atlantic
hordes arrived from near and far
seeking you out

your lyrics were simple
your arms soft
you were the rainbow city

jinns sneaked into your streets
to feast on your joy
to drink your sweet waters

your adorable face now has a deep scar
your memory is shredded like a soiled letter of divorce
now the city of saints has a monster's soul

the palliative waters of your clean beaches
that cured distressed souls are littered
and stink like a rapist's semen

the hermitage of saints, wayfarers,
migrant labourers and the lost
has turned into an anthem of pain and murder

the fabled Island of Banjullo
your dignity is buried deep
in sterile sands of your beaches

o' graceful dame
your back is hunched
your destiny dwarfed

the river Gambia quietly flows into the Atlantic
shedding tears over your fading glory
reckless regime change and festering poverty.

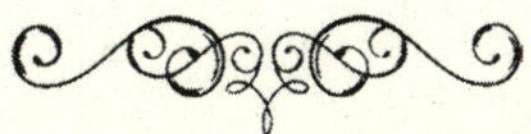

BISSAU

Drumbeat at Night

By Tony Tcheka

Bissau grows
when the sun shrinks
it comes with the night's thread
and only goes to sleep
when dawn breaks

Alcohol
and the weekend
inflame bodies
covered in adornments

At night
there's insomnias
and somnias of many names
it's not just the motto
here there's funk
there's merengue
and Antilleans in the middle of the night
Gusts of love
mold bodies
sweaty with passion
there is a permanent
dancing
on the night's catwalk
floating silks
thighs fidgeting
to a *sincopado*
with syncope

The scent
chews the air

stink
chanel
paco rabane
smelly water
sweat
and dior
unabashedly mingle
confuse themselves
ça va comme ça...
Old scotch
gives the finishing touch
It's fatal
eventually why not...

The drumbeat grows
opens up space
the city doesn't sleep

—*Translated from the Portuguese by* David Shook

BRAZZAVILLE

Dreaming of Brazzaville

By Aimé Eyengue

A dream
Far from town
Nearer to Brazzaville
Still in my veins
Flows the sound of this town
Wherever I am, from wherever I come
It's my cymbal call that

Girds my loins and brandishes its drum
Stirring my memories with its fresh waters
Spelling out its nick-name as Brazza-the-Green River City
Pouting into my dreams
Shaking my sleepy ear drums
Cuddling my neck with its memories
And I wake up with my feet in water.

—*Translated from French by* Christopher Macann

BUJUMBURA

Buyenzi, Bujumbura

By Abdoul Mtoka

Buyenzi, where I was born
Neighborhood far from here
Do you want to hear about it?
Please sit, and I'll paint you a picture.

See every road
They are twenty-five
So straight are the roads
You'd think they'd agreed to it,

I also see the Ndahangwa River
It slides into Lake Tanganyika,
And there are citrus trees, too
They're scattered now,

I see coconuts over there
Standing upright
Near us, palm trees
Shiny as rings,

See the mosques
Their tall towers
Brandished like breasts
Pale with light,

Now I see classrooms
And there are the teachers
Not a place for luxuries
It is the source of knowledge,

I see many children
They are playing ball

And those learning the basics
They are building thoughts,

I see mothers
Dressed in their kanga
And they feel no hostility
They don't need to bicker,

I also see the elderly
Already dressed in their vikoyi
Clean dresses and hats
They are sitting in the shade,

I even see mechanics
They do their work
And there are many categories
Of these, our residents,

Look at them and guess
And the other schools
Children are running
Without regarding the crosswalk,

My quarter, Buyenzi
You have the flower's perfume
And the moon's best light
And the sweetness of sweetmeat,

May I have the good luck
Of walking there again
Of sitting quietly
Of getting to rest again,

Buyenzi has beauty
Although people do not see it
It has a classic personality
I carry it in my heart.

—*Translated from the Swahili by* Jean Claude Nduwimana and David Shook

CAIRO

Road to Al-Qahira

By Matthew Shenoda

in memory, Cairo is a pomegranate
born of the fertility that bursts from her river

her streets glow like marrow in bone
shaped from fragments

frayed with the grit of time
aged is her heart

alleys that ache with empty bellies
and smile with eyes carved from sandstone

God bless the city
and the children in her breast

torsos wrapped in cloth
no telling what kind of song their chests sing

expanding like the ribs of your swollen wrists
we don't speak these things

they exist
like a tree gnarled by wind

when people rise from where they stand
stretch themselves closer to sky

they begin to see things from another angle
water becomes stone, water becomes light

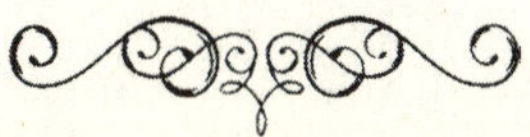

on these streets
a spirit made of human thread

learns to pull apart the past
and watch it flower in sand

only then will we cut something green
only then will we cut something fresh.

CAIRO

Progression

By Inara Cedrins

I.
In Cairo, clasped hands
we walk the streets numb —
the embassy will not allow us to marry,
you are not allowed into my hotel,
the clubs alongside the Nile
are all private, there is nowhere
for us to go. I swear to you
I will come back:

we'll stay at a hotel with more stars
than there are in the sky. I fly
back to my winter the next day,
there is no choice. Circumstance
makes me helpless.
I want to come back, to re
turn, like the ornate curlicues
over the mosque doors –

to bold and blaze
a kaleidoscope of color,
defiance of space. You write
I send you kisses
more than stars in the sky
but not soon enough.

II.
I return to marry someone else,
taking him to the embassy window
as though the men were interchangeable

as foil wrapped chocolates, saying again:
I wish to marry this Egyptian!
But this time prepared, though the papers
take weeks to translate, to stamp
with colored seals. The bribe-takers,
the lawyers, are all corpulent:

my love, we are betrayed
like the plundered bulls that lie in the vaults
at Saqquara, their golden casings
stolen by priests, one granite coffin
abandoned askew at the cavernous door, its removal
attempted for use as a president's bier.

This is nothing to do with us. For two months
I am trapped in these streets, restless
though fed pigeon stuffed with corn, sweet mango.
Netted oranges hang heavy in street alcoves.
I take him to the embassy
but your impress is on me
like an indentation on bruised fruit.

III.
The first part of the marriage
is performed in the sheesha cafe
where I am surrounded by men in filthy galabijas
that despise me. The fat lawyer says abruptly
repeat these words after me, say them
to him: and my husband's eyes go warm black
as I speak the Arabic delivering myself
into his hands. *Is this like one of the three*
life stages for lotus? in which it suffuses first pink,
then blanches to pure white. Afterwards we drink the sticky
hibiscus flower tea, karkadey, and go hand in hand
down the packed mud street to the hotel
where they say, let us see the paper, before
letting us have a room together. Later on the roof

the braziers are lighted, the air shimmers, it is
beyond hot. We drink Stella beer and have a sheesha
with the special apple tobacco, and our witness
who has the profile of a Roman senator, says to me
you make everyone around you respect you,
I love you like a sister. Later
the electricity's turned off in his home
and he asks for a loan.

IV.
All the signatures are gathered,
the colored stamps: *my friend adopted a baby*
from Peru and all the documents
had to be tied up with red ribbons.
They say in three months
the court will vote on whether we can marry;
when I expostulate, my husband
says I do not understand Egyptian law. Still
you're fused with me, like a body on a frieze
delineated in two lines
indicating two people fill that space.
It is only a transaction,
I never loved him. At what point
do you become irrecoverable, scattered,
like beads of quicksilver? In my mind
vaguely, long ago, a sequence
in which my mother said
when the thermometer broke, touch
the mercury with a silver spoon
and it'll form an alloy, cling. How long
can such a casing last? Indeed
you were like a fever. I know little
of many things. *I only*
loved you.

CAPE TOWN

A Prospect of Beauty and Unjustness
By Gabeba Baderoon

I walk down Heerengracht,
where pigeons dip their necks
like question marks into the fountain.
Then left at Long, while the sun slips

Toward the sea and the moon takes its place
above Signal Hill.
Above me, starlings clatter
like typewriters.

Higher still, turning right at Wale,
seagulls tilt like white kites
against the wind.

I step on the old silences of the city.

Here is the place on the hill where artists came
for peace and the view of the harbour.
Below, the city reveals itself.
We still walk the neat streets of their paintings.

Under the angled mountain, its blue light,
the starlings are cold but, looking at them,
I see the loveliness
of their chaotic and coordinated hunger.

What can explain
this exact and unjust beauty?

The flock clusters at sunset for warmth and seed.
Poetry cannot be afraid of this.

Sketching the streets, the artists stood
on the burial ground of the city's slaves.
In the paintings is something
of the private grief of their bodies.

In precise patterns the starlings follow one another
and redouble on their own flight-tracks,
slipstream of warmth,
blood-trace of the self.
Nothing to begin with,
and nothing again.

Around me, the air is thick with history.
Two hundred years ago,
slaves could no longer be sold.

Nothing, and nothing again.

I look again at the painted city, falling
silent at sunset, even the birds stilled.
In the last flash of the sun, the city gleams
white and hard as bone.

CONAKRY

Conakry

By Gerard Noiret

I – TARMAC

The famous mannequin who comes back – literally – as a deity
refusing to accept the compliments of the flight commander
forcibly soldiered out in the cabin
By the heat! The overpowering heat
Near a grating, at the end of the runway, you see
Hidden ghosts in the landing gear.
Triumphant, they exalt
Don't they know one dies of cold at 10,000 metres
even when reaching for one's dreams?

No sooner down the ramp and you become
RICH, as you never were in Paris
WHITE heiress of a detestable history
HEROINE of serial stories followed each night by fifteen around a set
an ANCESTOR who exceeds life's expectation
WHO FORGOT TO INVENT SHADE IN THIS COUNTRY?

OPEN YOUR EYES
The interminable wall of breeze blocks along
the road shut off the camp
where thugs keep prisoners cooking under corrugated
iron roofs …
An insane sun never stops sketching
thousands and thousands of silhouettes at breakneck speed
Leprosy colonies haven't even learnt a construction could be
straight or intact or that its foundations, moreover, might have
defied the centuries

OPEN YOUR EYES
… Yellow taxis serve one of many possible way-stations
in this hell
but a smiling hell, all coloured, playful, a joking child
A large brown lizard with an orange collar, others with their
heads in armour
Ask on what other side of this hell they might have seen
you already.

get the one he loves to sit down there
At the edge of the ocean, a young boy stretched out on concrete
ignores the beach
Stained with oil. He dreams of sneaking into the luggage
compartment
Of an A330

– *Translated by* Christopher Macann

COTONOU

Cotonou

By Abhay K.

Zemidjans rush
across the *Ancien Pont Bridge*
to the cathedral of Cotonou—
a zebra in burgundy and white

A tiny fishing village
on the banks of the Oueme
flourished for centuries
under the kingdom of Dahomey

with the King Ghezo´s blessings
the French set up a trading post
and a city rose
by the river of death.

Zemidjans Motorcycle-taxis

DAKAR

Piano Lessons

By Mildred K. Barya

I. Piano lessons

This happens in the sands of Dakar, Senegal. My teacher, Barry, is good, kind and solid. I begin to think how wonderful it would actually be to learn how to play in this coastal city. How many feet of the waterline, I want to ask. Barry tells me to pay attention to the intervals and feeling. After an hour, he prepares to leave and asks if I am not afraid to be alone. I tell him I'm getting used to it. The muezzin's call, kora music from the boutiques, bleating sheep on the streets, and cows crossing the road by the office window where I work, are invitations on how not to be. Alone. He advises that I should get an eye at the door to look into when someone knocks. I tell him I don't open the door if I do not know the person. He says that's even better. I must appear vulnerable to him. He is very vulnerable to me.

II. More piano lessons

The majors and minors can be mixed; anything can be played so long as you master the rules. You can even play on the border and between the rules. On edge. I like that very much. It excites my body, my fingers, and warms my heart. 'Once you begin to feel the music, you can play your own thing. It's about feeling, interval, rules.' It all sounds familiar.

DAR ES SALAAM

Memories of Dar es Salaam

By Charlotte Hill O'Neal

Charcoal smell wraps 'round *makaa* coals
sizzling and fizzling and assaulting my nostrils
with acrid sweet odors that I will never forget
Smells that always bring me memories of Dar es Salaam

Nerve jarring chalk-on-blackboard
screeching sounds
of welded scrap iron braziers
Sliding 'cross potholed cement floors

Wananchi stoves set out in optimum positions
to catch oddly timed morning breezes blowing through
fastidiously swept sandy courtyards
and third floor cemented stoops

Jiko stoves put in place by mamas and daughters
who fan ash rimmed pieces of charred wood to life
making them dance in red embers
and smoke rises up as a tendril

Women squat on low stools fanning back and forth
using fascinating implements to get the fires going
like bucket lids, cut out pieces of debe metal
and salvaged squares of old worn out mkeka

Nothing is thrown away, everything is put to use
much before recycling became a popular thing to do
Rhythmic sounds of narrow, carved rolling pins
and the beat of chapati making

over and over, thinner and thinner
the *chapati* circles grow
and is dipped into foamy, heavily spiced *masala chai*
poured from tall soldered brass pots

Black crows walk around fearless as they own it all
with their belligerent cries and suspicious bitter eyes
waiting to fly off with *chapati* crumbs
and pilfered *mandazi* skins

Old women carry heavy loads
of stiff green bananas
they ride on circles of faded *khanga* cloth
like weighty crowns on their heads

I see them competing jovially
with star-eyed young men
who carry freshly caught fish in plastic strings
with the smell of the ocean still clinging to their fins

Fresh, ambitious, full of possibilities
hidden in the belly of *mjini mkubwa* —Dar es Salaam
and the *muezzein* call wraps around it all
like heavy blues sounding parentheses

All encompassing, hot, muggy
rotten fish smell from the ocean
lapping hungrily at my toes
piercing the depth of my memories.

Makaa	charcoal
Wanachi	people
Jiko	metal cook stove that uses makaa or wood as fuel
Debe	container that can be metal or plastic...also used for a measurement, e.g. a debe of cooking oil
Mkeka	woven mat usually made from palm fronds/leaves

Chapati	an unleavened pancake like bread that is cooked on top of the stove. Popularized by the Indian community
Chai	tea
Masala	a mixture of spices used in tea and cooking
Mandazi	a doughnut-like fried bread
Khanga	a cloth commonly used in East Africa characterized by a border design and written proverb
Mjini mkubwa	big city

DJIBOUTI

Djibouti

By Abhay K.

Locked in the horn of Africa
the land of Issa and Afar
to ancient Egyptians—Punt
—the God's land ruled by Pharao

I have seen the powers come and go
the time's eternal ebb and flow
and who can say with certainty
what will happen tomorrow

but I have learned the sum of balance well
and keep my eyes and ears open
I know I'll manage to survive
long after fate of many nations are sealed

without a blink I watch over
the world's busiest sea lanes
jealously guarding access
to the Red Sea and the Indian Ocean.

FREETOWN

Freetown

By Steven J. Fowler

arm the East coast of Africa with kettles & steyr augs
train them aim & coral runs in claymore evade
for the West is arming Barrack tonnes & dodge
biscuits support a muscle / nervous system veind
with ring and lines as amuntion instows & docks
developing economic stocks in twelve British univsities
the shocks them loose. trains them to let loose
sight declines in civil wage strike between black factions
in the jewel getting it over with quicker because of the embedded
stick & noose & bause they are bloody tame, burns that show
white fat under a leak press mouth to a shell & blew on seven
beaches little with pellets, Greene, Brazil leaf from the breaches
Mexico over Sierra to rob the tourists who hadn't stayed indoors
the bottom of a well planning to wait out occupation but keep
coming underneath all ways easier
the hunger for oarrooks moments of mean
palm pill seer of the midday retracted kept coils
of a blackway of your reward
whether willing or not left virtue in that wall
am child I but known enough the teeth of children
to know preventative measure against future infidelities

GABORONE

Trying To Fit In

By Abhay K.

Between the hills of Kgale and Oodi
laid out like a glass of brandy

a city tries to fit in badly
along with its *Naledi*

Precious Ramotswe solves mysteries
in *Mmegi* and the Botswana Gazette

while the culprits flee to jungles of Mokolodi
in wagons, sledges and bakkies

the three *Dikgosi* close their eyes
and a tired Gaborone lets out silent cries.

Naledi Stars and a suburb of Gaborone
Mmegi A leading newspaper
Dikgosi A Chief

HARARE

Harare – The Sunshine City

By Chirikure Chirikure

We had our own name for the area, from time immemorial
Until the day colonizers came and took control of our fate
Building their monumental structures on top of our shrines
And gave the place a new name, in honour of their ancestors

We lived with that, until we gathered enough strength
And took back our heritage shading blood
We renamed it Harare once again as it was always known
But retaining its colonial nickname —the Sunshine City

Decades later, some plaques and mantels display boldly
Adverts float daily calling it Salisbury
Colonial ghosts cling on, unable to reverse the time
We move on unconsciously gloating over the sunshine

While the sun above Harare gets dimmer each day
Choked by poverty and squalor in the ghettos.

JUBA

Juba

By Abhay K.

The hill *Jebel Kujur* watches the old Nile
flow silently through the new capital

who could think the Greeks founded Juba
at a place infested with strife and malaria

they turned it into a bustling trade post
linking *DRC*, Uganda and Kenya

and when they had to go, they left behind
their quarters, markets and *Hai Jalaba*

now everything is under construction here—
a new road, a new airport, a new soul.

Jebel Kujur	A rocky hill just outside Juba
DRC	Democratic Republic of Congo
Hai Jalaba	A Greek suburb of Juba

KAMPALA

The City of the Antelope

By Mildred K. Barya

On arrival
the Europeans asked —
'what place is it
hilly and full of impalas?'

the antelope is missing
from the national air
there's a flag instead
with a crested crane in a white disc

the city led on to cities
evolving, dissolving
shape shifting, multiplying
sprawling beyond the seven hills

then lunatics plunged the city in chaos
blood flowed in hills, rivers and valleys
in alleys where people once danced
and made love, fled crying

those who lived to see another day
cannot recognize the city
new dreams take shape
there will be another city

growing in concentric circles
pushing in and out
eating its placenta
expelling it out.

KAMPALA

Kampala is a Display Window

By Beverley Nambozo Nsengiyunva

Our neighbours are always washing
new clothes. Even though they wear
the same ones every day. Like the
familiar jokes after the 9 o'clock news.
Their mother raises her voice whenever
she comes to borrow pegs.

'My son in Thailand has just sent us new
clothes. I have to soak them in softener.
Give me some pegs.'

While she hangs her new clothes she tells
me to have all my children at once. Having
children is like a relay race in Kampala.
She was passing on the 'having children at
once baton' to me.

The soapy water drips from the clothes.
But it doesn't wash away the lies.

'When are you going to tell your mother?
I ask her daughter,
the third child of the 'having children
at once project.'

'When are you going to tell your mother
That your brother is living with a rich
Muzungu man in *Naguru*.
and that those clothes belong to
the man's grandchildren?

**Muzungu means a white person*
Naguru is a high end suburb in Kampala

KHARTOUM

The Blue and the White

By Tim Cummings

The perch of the Blue Nile
is sweeter than the White.
We stepped ashore on the edge
of night to the moored
pleasure boat of an
undetermined time zone,

face of Kush in the three hashish
smokers sitting by the water,
idling under a cotton canopy,
civilising nightfall, this face
of the earth cooling by slow degree
back to the ochre of origin,

the oldest human mixer
a shell for imagination
and the Dog Star's progression,
cattle nosing from the cave wall
onto the banks of the Nile where
Blue meets White,

the smooth pale waters of one
rolling in the arms of the other,
bending a milky shoulder
through pyramids and night music,
the kingdom of Kush scattering
its boats across a glittering downriver.

Time moves like grain through wood,
memory opening up like a palm,

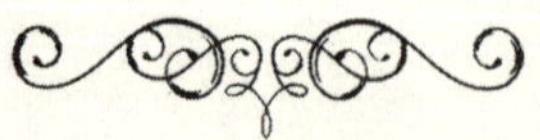

fermenting in buckets for moonshine
booze that scrambles the eyes
of old men squatting in the heat
of the sun, generous in its embrace,

heavy as a royal lineage, ancient dynasties
striking a coin from your face, the new breeze
scented with acacia blossom.
The three men on their haunches test
the strength of the heat, unfolding time
as if it came to its feet with directions
and a map, sunny side up, their onlooking
faces beaten flat as Bronze Age tin,
basking in the heat of a sun god
sinking back to a seafaring kingdom,
a rabbit song gutted for the pot,
artisans of the instructional proletariat

watching from the shoreline,
the stone age orchestra of mind's
fertile crescent hung like figs
under dark green leaves. Now
close your eyes. Clouds of
smoke obscure the sun

and deliver us, pressing semi-
erect flesh against the fabric
of Omdurman souq at dusk, kid
goats hung from steel hooks
over the butcher's radio,
the Koranic singer's voice

falling like folded silk across
the verses, the shoe souk strung
out like junk DNA, alley after
alley, Kerosene lamps and insect swarms

like meteor storms, milky nebulae
fusing stars from blind matter,

the smoking plasma of black coffee
a women with a face like the sun
hands you on a silver tray, the element
that fixes you like solder or chewing gum
to the moment you're in, the dark matter
of traffic and trade swimming to the bright lights,

every movement an undoing, the moon
hung over our side of the planet, hand-held
time working its loom, the air charged
with horse electricity and a simple melody,
little chords, nothing fancy but the feeling
and the promise that keeps its word.

KIGALI

Seasons of My City

By Sitawa Namwalie

My city is a mirror of shifting moods,
A place of heaving seasons.
Sometimes she may disturb,
Mostly she will fascinate and please.
Today my city is a striking woman
Beauty stepping out in splendour,
Leaving gaping admiration in her wake.

At other times she is like a man
With a large beer belly, lumbering;
Floppy man-boobies flapping in the wind,
Hot, heavy and significant.
The day tires easily.

Then she gets moody for months
Like a menopausal woman,
Bad tempered and disconnected.
She turns grey and cold,
Sulking under a foreboding sky;
She doesn't know herself.
We fold in on ourselves,
Wait for her mood to change,
Hoping we won't be found out,
Bear the brunt of a withering tongue-lashing.

And then again she morphs
Into a young girl, nubile and vain,
Changing hair styles to entice an impatient lover.
Brilliant butterflies hover like perfume:
Orange, yellow-green, iridescent-blue

Purple and red.
The young spring day pops buds of jade,
Ageless in its beauty

Suddenly, she takes on the hue of new lovers
Caught in an upset quarrel. Faces thunderous,
They cry bitter tears of passion.
Hiding, we run for cover to avoid getting drenched.
The rain refreshes and makes everything new.
Sometimes my city is a thief,
Who comes like a starless night,
Inky black and filled with apprehension.
She is out to steal your heart.
If you're not careful,
You will fall in love and never leave.

KINSHASA

Mbote, Kinshasa

By Annie Finch

Kinshasa, warm city spread out and alive,
night-dark in rich silence, bird-bright in rich sun,
Kinshasa, deep heartbeat, strong, ready to give,
Kinshasa, the many, Kinshasa, the one.

Night-dark in rich silence, bird-bright in rich sun,
you nourish the voices your country will need.
Kinshasa, the many, Kinshasa, the one,
you offer the stars of your brightness like seed.

You nourish the voices your country will need,
Kinshasa, warm city spread out and alive;
you offer the stars of your brightness like seed,
Kinshasa, the many, Kinshasa, the one.

LIBREVILLE

Libreville
By Abhay K.

Vast gated villas, well laid out streets
pavements—spick and span
welcome to the capital of Gabon

a tiny trading post is now half the nation
with sculptures twenty feet tall
at the sea front facing the Atlantic ocean

at night the city comes alive at Louis town
and over a drink people at times remember
the fifty-two slaves who were freed here.

LILONGWE

Bird-Watching In Lilongwe

By Frank M. Chipasula

I: The Birds

In a new season the wings vary
as to span and hue of feather, orange
fading into yellow, green browning under
the heavy pressure of the dark truth,
red panicking away from spilt blood.

In the eaves of the whitewashed
dungeons, kindred divide shredded prey
while lesser beggar birds line the streets
below in tattered wings and open their feeble
beaks to sing for meager morsels.

Constant the clutching claw,
the borrowed light that polishes
their feathers and adds luster
to their voracious beaks, for all
seek the same worm on the dunghill.

II: The Hill

Crows, eagles, hawks and vultures
nest in the same fiery Cashgate trees
where bluebirds hide their juicy worms
in abandoned bloated leather bellies
loaded with enough morsels to feed
the million orphaned scrawny chicks.
To beak and claw they all agree
on clout to claw out a watchful eye
but leave a smoke stain on quizzical skin.

III: The City's Two Faces

Though the white city curses the black
in fluent Afrikaans, it stutters on the bird-
lime of Mandarin and carefully broken English,
colorful in masquerades, here where East
meets West and South in dark deeds-

The soft loans simmer still and rise as dough
with each cockcrow, while the eagle's talons
sink into the bluebirds' bulging necks
as their voracious beaks suck our souls.
In these myth-stained streets
where a gaunt lion once roamed
with a specific limp that a cane
could not tame, now stroll blue-
birds, once dyed yellow, stopping
to whet their obdurate beaks
on the rough zebra sidewalks where

they smashed raw mangoes retching
ochre-tainted sap and well-repressed
thoughts they could not mouth even
beneath the silence draped over the praise
songs that wiggled loose, well-oiled snake-
hips a flywhisk failed to paralyze or sedate.

III: Heroes' Acre

In this acre of defeated heroes, a despot
stuck in concrete, metal and stone,
lashes at the winds that strike his ego;
for this toy city he sold his pride,
learnt to crow low and lick a boot to shine.

He scraped and shrank himself into a midget,
shook the devil's hoof for a few rotten rand

to raise a mausoleum to crass lunacy
and hold up his crumbling cornerstones
ready to drop them on any coconut head.
Now bird lime graces his generous nose.

IV: The New City

The city cowers under the jacaranda flower
showers, the birds of paradise, the flame trees,
the sad bougainvillea, the loud hibiscus, the armpits
of the polished rainbow, the rose baring its honest
thorns, from apartheid's group dirty areas acts.

After the bird-watching I will fling wide open
the green city's gates, flush out the foul light,
and let the newborn sun and dove stride in.

LOME

Night In Lomé

By Meg Pierce

As the sun sinks into
rooftops over Ghana
the heaviness of the heat lifts.
Clouds gather in the dusk,
while veined black wings
decorate the grumbling gray
with sonar-guided silhouettes.

I face death by moto,
perching here, a valet
between my thighs,
pointing our two wheels
towards the oncoming truck,
playing chicken on our way
around the roadblock.

Dozens of Cyclops eyes
pierce through the drowsy
lids of darkness closing in.
Honk! Beep! Zoom! Squeal!
As the sun slips into slumber
the city wakens in a frenzy.

Blues at the Galion –
songs to sing to.
Beer on the boulevard –
buy your cigarettes,
condoms or viagra.
Language, laughing, lounging.

Dancing! The club,
the crowded hub of bodies
moving to the music,
reenacting ancient forms
of celebrations, prayers,
calls to gods and war.

The din of night,
meanders into early morn.
Under the motionless,
moonlit sky a lone moto
hums along, silently scattering
plastic scraps. I yawn.

LUANDA

Luanda

By Abhay K.

A city of contrasts, crammed to the hilt
heat, dust, squalor, filth
sky-rocketing prices

multitude of shacks, high rises
a heave of sigh at the Marginal
after twenty seven years of civil war

a whitewashed Portuguese fort
perched on the hill
watches the city heal.

LUSAKA

What Is Left of Africa

By Jekwu Ozoemene

The angry effulgent African sun
Stares me down
Along Middle way Kabulonga
An orderly simulacrum of an English neighbourhood
Lined with luxuriating green leafed trees
Not the symmetry you will find in Africa he sighs
Far from the chaos you'll find in Lagos

My early morning walk briefly interrupted
By his laser like rays examining my thoughts
The intensity of his words scalds me
As my core briefly confluences with the raging furnace of his soul

Whose sun am I anyway, he muses
Then blazes at me, red rays' fiery darts of pity
Searching for the Africa that is left in me
The Lusaka that is left in Kabulonga

You are the sun of Africa I retort defiantly
Hieratic clenched right fist shaking at the radiance of his doubts
The sun of Lagos and Lusaka!
You are our sun! I shout, angrily thumping my chest

Yet he smiles
Sagely
His whispered response barely audible
Look at you, he sighs
Walking down an English Road in Lusaka
Whose son are you?
Before I could muster an appropriate response

He mockingly slips away
Sagely
Still resplendent behind the luxuriant boughs of the tree lined street
In what is left of Africa in Lusaka.

MALABO

Mini-topography of Santa Isabel

By Marcelo Ensema Nsang

Plaza De Espana

The tired afternoon falls
on a rhythm of palm trees
clad in spring
human, a scattered voice.
Above, the moon rounds
its silver & enamoured
spins its gratitude
– starry light swerves
between the coupling of harnesses –
through gothic cypresses
that toll the bells.

Market

Rivers of joy full of the very thing
played only by this Stradivarius of beings
trampoline that launches us from the pole
of artifice to pristine contact
with the virgin, packed bustle
of naked Africa... Protocol
of baskets & tables, bloodclots, deceit,
yucca & the solemn fraternity in the act
of being emptied and filled in between laughter
drawing coins without currency,
rain of ancient sun on their backs.
Lean out – by the skin of the day –
into that open custom of exchange,
a life running among skirts.

Point Cristina & Point Fernanda

Album of doves
that comes to coo
the sister couple
who sleep in the sea.
The air in the trees
starts to play
at being mime & comb
kiss & madrigal.
Light. Calm. Silence.
Waves, nothing more.
... & the two sisters,
wives of the sea.
(1967)

Elegy In Stone

I speak to you of my destiny when I die,
one afternoon, beside the virgin fountain,
at the edge
of my final memory.
I hope you will say:
'His life was to a stone
as a song is to a lark. Exactly.
You left it to the alien mime
& the spark jumped – flint –
of a hollow smile
withering at its core.
He offered you his life, firm on the platter
of his friendship, full of itself, yes, to the very brim.
You had to tell him: 'This is heavy'
& your hands gave out under the bulk
to the tug of the earth.'
'Take my life' – he said to you – 'beneath the flesh of my easy smile'.
Then his life was a dry leaf

in the arms of the wind...
You will also say: 'On his shoulders the heads
of friends stumbled over the edge
of fierceness...'
Later you'll fling me
– like a stone –
to the heart of oblivion.
& I will live out the sentence
I will die standing like the trees
I will leave this opaque dolmen that I am
planted in the earth.

& I will stay standing
numb
alone
like a stone.

—*Translated by* David Shook

MAPUTO

Maputo

By Abhay K.

No one really knows
what Maputo means
it is just the name of a river

that lends its name to the city
of acacias, jacarandas and flames
of lush tropical gardens

the proverbial pearl of the Indian ocean
is dotted with old colonial palaces
and Stalinist concrete boxes

a tuk-tuk, a chapa to Museu or baixa
Galabiyya-garbed men sell bananas
women wrapped in colourful *capulanas*

local fishermen are lost listening to Radio
near the metal-plated curiosity — Casa do Ferro
Maputo may mean a stroll at Catembe or Ponta d'Ouro.

MASERU

Maseru, Love

By Rethabile Masilo

Once, when winter was refusing to leave
and spring could not push it out, and never
could a season stay as long as that,
I spent days on Kingsway sitting on the street railing,
watching children shuffle
in search of work parking cars; I spent days there
with my heart's chimera
pointed at such questions. And so it was that one winter
I finally withdrew into its sea,
as spring bounced to touch the mountains,
and took one home with me, and made him heir
to what my lifetime had collected in solitude.

MBABANE-LOBAMBA

Mbabane-Lobamba

By Abhay K.

To Hhohho
to Mbabane, to Lobamba
along the river Polinjane
and the mountains of Mdzimba
through cool high veld Ezulwini
to the Royal Kraal
bow to the queen mother Ntombi
dance Incwala and Umhlanga.

Kraal	enclosure
Umhlanga	Reed Dance

MOGADISHU

Landscape Genocide

By Ladan Osman

I slept thinking of Lido beach, how my mother walked there
every morning when pregnant with me. I know the mineral scent
of seawater wherever I am. If the sun bakes the metal of earth,
if my own damp scalp sweats, if I hold my hennaed palms
to my face. I have said, 'God. There is no god but God'
into my metallic palms. When my blood started, war started.
Ever since the war started, I dye a henna disk on each palm.
I refresh it when it browns, old blood. 'God,' into my mineral
palms when the whole street was white sheets, thin men
digging graves night til dawn til night til dawn. They paused
for every single prayer. I woke thinking of an orb of light.
It dragged me through a dim street. It lifted me off my feet.
I shouted 'This is my light!' and held it tight against my belly.
I was still, beyond known stillness, a gravity of my own,
and still I didn't light the street. I woke thinking of Lido beach.
The last thing my mother promised me was a photo of her,
five months pregnant, at the shore, backlit by the ocean.
'Go at dawn,' she'd say. The water was warmest at dawn.
At dawn, girls went to the sea in whatever they were wearing,
even if they had school later. Their mothers couldn't keep them
from the water, from walking fully dressed into it.
I woke up thinking there was nowhere to go but Lido,
that the orb, a giant marble in my diaphragm, would float
with me there. There was nowhere to go but into the sea.
Between this interior desert and the sea at the edge
of my known world, orange pekoe tinted sand
marked with the heels and balls of firm and dazed feet.
Charred acacias face down in the dust. Succulents
marking clusters of graves. Graves of people
and fruit-bearing trees. Bones of tall livestock,

the startling domes of camel ribs lit like a great hall
by the relentless sun. There is nowhere to go but the sea.
Between here and its mineral scent, bones of people,
small and not small, bush lions and their young,
always litters of bones at the line between known
and wild worlds. Between here and Lido, the land
in full prostration. The only song, metallic. Shells,
or whole bullets underfoot, sometimes whole piles
at the edge and center of towns put facedown
at night, at dawn, during afternoon prayer, at dusk.
Between here and Lido, the land and everything
in it, in full submission to the mineral scent
of our water and blood and inability to cry anything,
not even 'God! No god but God!' We go at dawn.

MONROVIA

Monrovia

By James V. Dwalu

The city of bliss
the Atlantic washes your feet
the sneaking Mesu ripples
around the Providence
where the Elizabeth docked in 1822

J. J. Roberts stands on Ducor Hill staring
the place from where he led
once the nation of the free
he looks at the Trinity Cathedral
where we say our prayers to the Lord

Ducor to Cape Mesurado to Christopolis
the namesake of James Monroe since 1824
on the Broad Street
flamboyant trees form a queue
tiny red flowers lure folks from the countryside

August rain gushes down like angry gods
flooding Broad, Benson, Carey and all
street urchins chase cars everyday
yelling the names of places
we would like to go.

MORONI

Moroni
By Abhay K.

In the heart of fire
at the foot of Mount Karthala
boats are moored in the harbour
and children swim in the Indian Ocean

the setting sun paints the sky
crimson and the chirp of birds
mixes with the sound of prayers
from the *Ancienne Mosquée*

giant fruit bats hover above my head
I rush through a maze
of narrow streets in the old Medina
seeking serenity of turquoise.

N'DJEMENA

N'Djemena

By Zaharaddeen Ibrahim Kallah

I flew over the rivers Longone and Chari
past the Zakounta National Park
listening to the whistling of Chagoua and Mbololo
relishing sparkles of the Paris Congo
Moursal and Avenue de Charles-de-Gaulle

blood changed the colour of the city
the fire of hatred destroyed it
but it could not destroy N'Djemena's spirit
it healed after prolonged bloodsheds and conflicts
And once again is back on its feet.

NAIROBI

Portrait

By Ngwatilo Mawiyoo

For Nairobi

I

And I am the dust that has no place,
that lines the walls, leaves. Waits
for rain, dreads it, waits: flees.

II

Daily, almost daily a woman –
a man – wipes a floor;
head down, bottom high,
shuffling, pivoting in swirls,
left right and back, the path
of a clean woman, a good woman –
the man only a faithful servant erasing

III

He is in the ground, bones
ensconced in sateen. It lined
a smoothed tree. There
are the plastic handles, gold
you grasped
when you bore him to the hole.

IV

For both sides of Tom Mboya
street, shrouds that will not rot.
For dust that will not stay away
telling what we buried alive
calling to grass, to acacia,
to cool water.

NIAMEY

Niamey

By Yusuf Adamu

I

Even when the great River Niger beckons us
Your glorious sunset waves its golden hands
Last gate Gendarmerie spoils our smiles
And we bear the hostile angst of robots
By dawn we drive into your wide palms

II

Across the two tablelands dividing the city
I traverse the classic *Ganti Yena* Stream
In this city of contrasts, the city of segregation
I breathe the scent of Hausaland in Zango
In this brownish city of lower and upper markets
I see the new capital refusing to see its face
In the mirror of the river Niger

NOUAKCHOTT

Nouakchott

By Abhay K.

A reddish Martian flatland in the middle of the desert
haunted by winds, shifting sand dunes and droughts

a caravan stop from the sea port of Atlantic
strange, sleepy, unassuming, laid-back, idiosyncratic,

somewhat urban, somewhat nomadic
intricate streets, one-storeyed buildings

the grand mosque rises like the full moon over the city
scores of tourists treasure hunt for Saharan meteorites

fishermen arrive in brightly painted sea canoes
donkey carts ply on the road loaded with fish

passing through overflowing Kebbes, frantic markets
nomads relocate—a city migrates within a city.

Kebbes concrete shanty towns

OUAGADOUGOU

Ouagadougou

By Andy Knowlton

Joe the accountant is beyond suicidal,
which sounds
like he might be dead, which he almost is
but not quite yet.

He goes to the office on Friday
wearing a red bowtie and nothing else
and he hands out Xerox copies
of his ass to everyone including his boss
and his boss says what the hell are you doing
and Joe says, I'm quitting, duh.

He goes home with the plan to throw a dart
at his map and travel wherever the dart lands
and he secretly is aiming for Australia,
but it is a small map and so
he hits Ouagadougou in Burkina Faso.

Since the map is small, it just says 'Oua.'
and 'Burka Fa' and Joe doesn't know what to do.

PORT LOUIS

A Taxi Driver's Chat From Port Louis to Roche Bois

By Saradha Soobrayen

'Come... get in, safest, fastest, cleanest car in *Porlwi*,
see, the Air Mauritius building, high rises on your right!

Oui, oui, Le Caudan Waterfront has the freshest Sushi
at the Attitude Sushi Bar, hold tight*, non, non,* red light!

Half a million! *Oui, oui,* indentured labourers at Aapravasi
Ghat, a first landing site, *oui, oui,* a World Heritage Site!

*Non,non...*conditions improved since the 19th century
under Gandhi's influence, *oui, oui,* workers put up a fair fight

Oui, oui, proud of the rainbow nation – the empire's legacy –
is never-ending for the *Ilois,* AKA the Chagossian, *non non,*right

of return to Chagos, next stop *Porlwi* dock, last stop slum city.
Lives upside down like *bol renversè. Oui, Oui nu* sleeping tight

in *Roche Bois*' a 'Mauritian Soweto', *non, non* another robbery
and *nu morisien* want progress, *oui, oui,* running water and light

'*Anu Amelyor Nu Kartier*' *oui, oui,* end to police brutality!
There are *non, non* international flights out of extreme poverty.'

PRAIA

Praia

By Abhay K.

A clandestine harbour
free of pirates and custom duties
myriad cannons guarding the city
and the monument
of the navigator Diogo Gomes

riot of colours in the streets
festive mood, celebrations
at the old city square
Praia readies itself to welcome
the Beagle and Charles Darwin.

RABAT

Rabat

By Abhay K.

Rabat sings its song
bouregreg bouregreg bouregreg
along the river bank
bouregreg bouregreg bouregreg

Moriscos drip as tears from Euope's eyes
into the Kasbah of the Udayas
once again Barbary pirates rise
in distant coastal lands a soul cries

storks build nests over the ruins
of Phoenician, Roman sovereigns
the mating pairs clack their bills
and women feed eggs to the eels

Rabat sings its song
bouregreg bouregreg bouregreg
along the river bank
bouregreg bouregreg bouregreg.

SAO TOME

Água Grande

By Conceição Lima

I´ll talk now about an ordinary river.
A river riddled with continental speeches.
An innermost river like the heart of the island.

Água Grande, not like the Congo, not like the Nile.
Água Grande with no canoes nor regattas, just a river
That meets the sea, her water fluid as fate.

But you, who knows all the cities.
You, a pilgrim, dweller of many rivers.
You don´t know the face of my city.
You don´t know the river embodied in my city.

Água Grande, beyond all your travels,
Just a river, sister of all rivers.

—*Translated by* Marcos Freitas

TRIPOLI

Tripoli

By Sabrina Masud

I, Google, the word Tripoli
And I, add words like, culture,
Myth, legend, next to – before –
And after Tripoli; images flood
My screen with Tripoli; bodies
Red and smoke, ash and almost
Audible ra-ta-ta-ta-tat, from Tripoli –
Lies in the womb of Mediterranean sea
A leech inside and a name, that is,
Tripoli, mated in Sanskrit, and Arabic
And Greek and the Romans who are gone
From the land of Tripoli; Rat-ta-ta-ta-tat;
Burns, a Tripoli, the olive lost in its travel
From *Khan-al-Saboun*, the coitus with
Honey, burnt, as patrol burns, in Tripoli.
And the Churches on Church Street,
Speak of crusades, and the Hammam
allows men, only, and the city burns
Irrespective of gender, tomb and I,
sigh, over the ice-cream that is also
centuries old and *Al Mina* stands
silent, her eyes gone sore from
dust that has gathered in the corners
before the medieval world echoed,
echoes,
rat-a-tat-a-tat 21st century Tripoli.

Khan-al-Saboun	Famous 18 century soup market
Al Mina	The legendary port that existed before medieval era

TUNIS

Tunis
By Abhay K.

I rest in the great heat of the desert
under the shadow of the Carthage

I hear the footsteps of the Roman soldiers
I hear the sound of carnage and destruction

as I wake up all alleys lead to ez-Zaytouna
I run through the narrow labyrinths of Medina

leaving behind the busy souqs
I rush out of the old town

to take a breath of fresh air
at the Avenue Habib Bourguiba

at the Ville Nouvelle, I find Hannibal
sauntering aimlessly, I say hello

he smiles and whispers in my ears—
how to cross the Alps.

VICTORIA

Victoria

By Abhay K.

Victoria reveals its secrets slowly, seductively, gently,
giant tortoises, parrot fish effuse the spirit of Seychelles

as the clock tower Little Ben in the city-centre strikes ten
people come out in the street, wearing the spirit of Seychelles

it is hard to miss colours in this hidden little tropical paradise
George Camille's paintings exude the spirit of Seychelles

mosque, temple, cathedral, emerald hills and turquoise sea
sandy beaches, coco del mar, all invoke the spirit of Seychelles.

WINDHOEK

Windhoek

By Abhay K.

In the *Khomas* highlands
in the heart of Namibia
where Africa meets Europe
castles puncture the skyline
and adventure begins

the *sudwester reiter* rises against the wind
on his Pegasus, flies past *tintenpalast*
admiring *christuskirche's* colourful stained glass
uttering 'Friede auf Erden'
—Peace on the Earth.

YAMOUSSOUKRO

Yamoussoukro

By Karla Brundage

With my mom
I had been here forty years ago
It was flat, dry and hot
How small and peaceful everything once was

How the sun set and how as a young girl
She snuck out at night
To meet a man with an alligator
We pass his descendants now

The alligator is caged
In the moat of the President's house
The wildlife is gone
No ivory is left in the Ivory Coast

It is cliché to tell young people
The elephants have gone
My students don't care
They want an i-phone 6

At the Basilica we are impressed
With its grandness
The community effort, the sacrifice
While the cross looms large above us

I cannot forget this land
That once produced coconuts
Now houses a shrine of the saviour
A present to Rome

I stand in Rome in Africa, they say
The greatest monument of Yamoussoukro
A gift to the Pope
Politely he should have declined

After all, they already took all the ivory
It has been paid for
Over and over again
What sins?

YAOUNDE

Sightseeing In Yaoundé

By Viola Allo

On the way to Yaoundé,
I fall asleep in my father's car,
as it glides over the curves
the road that weaves
in and out of the hills
and around the mountains
from Bamenda to Mbouda
to Bafoussam, through Banganté
and on to Yaoundé.
I fall sleep and miss the scenery,
when I wake up in Yaoundé,
I see a dirty, messy city
like every city I've seen
in Cameroon.

Only God can clean the mud off the walls.
I see piles of putrid refuse, rubbish
that no one knows what to do with.
I see children begging
outside the cinema hall
an infant and her mother
hungry, perhaps homeless,
sitting in front of the boulangerie-pâtisserie
I see tall fences and swimming pools
in suburbs like Bastos, houses with fresh coat
of paint, slick streets, gated embassies and
fortified residences where wealthy
Cameroonians and foreigners live.
I see lavish banks, skyscraper hotels and offices,
Mercedes cars rolling through the central roundabout.

I see the maddening mish-mash
of wealth and adversity, and
I squeeze my father's hand,
clamber back into his car and stay there.

AMERICAS

ASUNCION

Taxi Ride After Dark

By Gwen Burnyeat

At midnight traffic lights
All cars drive through red –
it's dangerous to stop.

Away from the centre
on unpaved streets, the driver swerves
round a pothole and we pass

the tall metal gates of the Country Club.
The armed guards in navy blue uniforms
notice us. They've not much else to do

in those yellow-lit huts.
One is eating a sandwich. What goes on
behind those iron gates?

I think of champagne bubbles
At fashion-designer weddings.
Guaraní folk music before *The Blue Danube* –

although most real *Guaraní* – like my driver –
listen to electronic *cumbia*
on pirate CDs

outside one-room breeze-block houses
amid white plastic chairs
on the city's fringes.

I think of Celia Cubas
ex-President's daughter, kidnapped
and held for six months

in an underground safe-house,
found beaten and starved to death.
The taxi driver doesn't feel like chatting.

Neither do I.I pay and get out.
I step round chipped cobbles
and head for the double-locked door.

BASSETERRE

Marcus Garvey Stood on Basseterre Bay Road

By Imruh Bakari

As with all comings
many would have claimed
to have seen the signs time
was already ticking
blood
was already boiling

messages had passed between
labourers and factory workers
potent songs were sung
by barefoot travellers and proud women
serving at high tables

The circus clock
was standing still
and going nowhere when Marcus Garvey
stood on Basseterre Bay Road
not far from the old slave
market in Pall Mall Square

His voice took the sea
breeze inland
where volcanic rock resides

He stood to speak
of citizens
He stood to speak
of hope

He stood to speak
of self-confidence

He stood to speak
of free will

He stood to speak
of duty and responsibility
He stood to speak
of self-expression and liberty

he spoke
of the ungodliness
that is inequality

here I stand
he said
because of my purpose

he spoke
of the devil
that is illiteracy

determined to leave
a mark more permanent
than the smell of fried fish

he spoke
of the hell
that is misery

the Mutual Improvement Society
Hall was packed
with the capacity for greatness

he spoke
of the prison
that is poverty

Nineteen thirty-seven
was a good year for cane fires
and better was supposed to come

Sharp machetes
had already
cleared a path

from Jamaica to Ethiopia
to the Cape and Cairo
across Harlem
to raise a flicker on Kilimanjaro

Among the gathered

where injustice had been
a constant visitor
and torn-up caps no shield
from torture
the black-star flag fluttered

But when Marcus Garvey stood
on Basseterre Bay Road he knew
there was much more
work to do

Threadbare after years of treachery
his words still rattled the circus clock
echoing across the slave market tombs
holding the blood-stained auction block

Like the sea breeze
that is always sure to become a hurricane
the weary rocked
on the wing of Marcus Garvey's refrain

fix-up you'self
fix-up you'self
fix-up you'self

BELMOPAN

Belmopan

By Abhay K.

The new capital of Belize was planned
like Canberra, Islamabad or Ottawa
on a highland away from the Caribbean

safe from the deadly tidal waves
where the river Belize meets Mopan
when a hurricane destroyed the old one

the new city square built with grey stones
its broad steps, a reminiscence,
a nostalgia of the Maya civilization.

BOGOTA

City at the Edge of Night

By Amparo Osorio

But the city still not founded encloses us
with one single mask
—Alfredo Silva Estrada

Like a swarm of fallen angels
the afternoon's reddish clouds descend
In the hollow of the city

begins the strange gravitation
of melancholy smoke

Who, tonight, will initiate the feast
scaring away
the indefinable light?

Who among your tallest eucalyptus
could weave the music of a saxophone?

Ah so much night
yet it is impossible
to meditate in silence

Because the dead drag to your shore
the moisture of their dreams
and their long chain of crystal beads.

– *Translated by* Luis Rafael Gálvez

BRASILIA

Brasilia, Candangós Land

By Marcos Freitas

The water fountain —
a sonorous light
wetting the feet of the TV tower.

Bulcãós blue bird
has got wings and freedom.
The project-city.

The submerged Amauri Village.
Everything looks so close,
but is so far away.

The city has to be seen through
the windows of cars and buildings
and amidst *cobogós*.

The city is built up with monuments
always-waiting-for-restoration.

Half a century of solitude
within the central highlands of the country.

Does the dangling cherubs blue church city bows its knees
before the four bells of Spain?

Does the gold-*pequi* dawn color city
lighten their mazes of empty spaces?
The city, an indigenous fire
that burns its contradictory bowels.

The city without traditions —
fire and water contradiction —
a bent plant, blue print, master plan.

The city of the new dreams
awakens inside me.

BRASILIA

Brasilia

By Abhay K.

'Between parallels 15 and 20,
around a lake which shall be formed;
A great civilization will thrive,
and that will be the Promised Land.'
— Don Bosco

Brasilia is mostly white
Brasilia is red laterite
Brasilia is diaphanous gossamer filled with light

Brasilia is a string of shining pearls at night
Brasilia is an exotic Turkish delight
Brasilia is a coiled serpent ready to bite

Brasilia is a village passing as a city
Brasilia is an expression in supernatural geometry
Brasilia is Italo Calvino's invisible city

Brasilia is a prophecy of Don (Bosco)
Brasilia is a poem carved in stone
Brasilia is a song of Carlos Drummond (de Andrade)

Brasilia is a diamond in the crown
Brasilia is a giant airplane on the ground
Brasilia is an Amauri village drowned

Brasilia is Clarice Lispector sleep-walking on water
Brasilia is black Acai palm dissert
Brasilia is perfection in brick and mortar

Brasilia is a piece of space cake
Brasilia is a fantasy island in the lake
Brasilia is a Dominican night shake

Brasilia is the last utopia
Brasilia is Sylvia Plath's dystopia
Brasilia is a landscape ectopia

Brasilia is an oasis of migratory birds
Brasilia is an oracle's prophetic words
Brasilia is a page from the Harry Potter

Brasilia is a shifting mirage in the desert
Brasilia is a vision gone pale, blurred
Brasilia is a nail yet to be hammered.

BRIDGETOWN

Spirit Bond; 1955, 2007

By Linda M. Deane

We claim the strip of balcony, the one that frames
the idle Wharf and overhangs the street—that well-oiled machine
with its tides. My father and me killing drinks with Time.

Inside, the Spirit Bond is sepia-memoried wall-to-wall.
Ground-floor arcade seeping, containing men and boys
wired to consoles while reality alternately crawls,

then races by outside—an endless series of signals, switches,
constraints and controls. Sun like a Collins, got everything
hacked in sharp relief, the Lewis-Wickham Boardwalk blinding.

I lef' Barbados from somewhere 'bout here…

My father proclaims with schoolboy wonder.
And next thing we ditching drinks and cool interiors,
our feet competing with the scorch of boardwalk

to where the City drops into the sea.
You can walk to the edge and drop 'way too,
like migrant workers fishing on evenings

dropping lines, or furtive couples dropping guard
by the picnic tables and on the benches. Passers-by
averting glances—all, somehow, on the edge.

Come, leh we walk there now…

And we walk there now, history leaping and pawing at us,
schooners and tug boats pulling—a generation ferried out
to the big ships waiting to steer them away

into distant steel-grey light. My father remembers
he was late the day he sailed: last minute haste
his brother driving, Speightstown to Bridgetown,

crazily; old man on a bicycle, wobbling: Narrow miss—
the suitcase spilling, his possessions clinging
to familiar soil—him, the last one on the tug,

The S.S. Hubert, past its point of no return already.

We stand now on solid ground, pathways
sculpted through the manicure of shrubbery
and street furniture. All here was water, he says.

At least, he thinks so. *Yeh, back then, this was ocean.*
I look to see the lines of hope decked in all its traveling best,
stretching far beyond the harbour, taking next steps.

Back at the Bond, we kill more Time—
another round and later, leave the way we came,
passing men and boys at ground level, still

Playing games at the edge of Bridgetown.

BUENOS AIRES

Casa Natal de Borges

...a man who, in an age that worships the chaotic idols of blood, earth and passion, preferred the lucid pleasures of thought and the secret adventures of order.

– Borges on Valéry

By Clive Wilmer

The secret adventures of order
Began in this emblem of the *Belle Epoque*:
The orderly elegance of the *haut-bourgeois*,
Who have secrets but few adventures.

Lost to its old seclusion, smeared with grime,
It endures quotidian rage, an inhuman alarm
And in shop windows intimacies laid bare.
It persists, though,
Like the last, yellowing, undecayed incisor
In a mouth whose gleaming beauty is long gone.

The city as *locus* of civility:
An accident of time perhaps? But time
Moves on and leaves behind it
An invisible city, continuing, made of messages
Strung together by those who have most cherished
The lucid pleasures of thought.

BUENOS AIRES

Looking for Borges in Buenos Aires

By Abhay K.

I know of one Greek labyrinth which is a single straight line.
Along that line so many philosophers have lost themselves.

– Borges

Looking for Borges
I came to Buenos Aires
I found him nowhere

I searched all the libraries
all the labyrinthine streets of the city
he was not even at La Recoleta

I found merely a mirror
and a face staring
at me in disbelief

it's hard to believe
everyone told me
Borges lived in Argentina.

CARACAS

The Ninth Floor In Caracas

By Marcela Sulak

In the streets below Draghitza's body
rain baubles the yellowish-brown light—

her body's wet and slick as street
and brown between the window slats—it´s rain-

ing and the pipes groan *porque*.
        She turns off
the faucet, reaches for the soap, suds

leave her hands and slide the way
stolen bulbs of light slide
        (on electrical lines
        diverted through the mountainside
        barrios, where it also rains,
        puddling the floor, baby slapping
        water and the hair-line cracks of concrete
        like the lines around Draghitza's mouth)

        (*I pay for my electricity*
        Franklin says, who lives there).

It´s raining
on her bright breasts, it´s raining on her belly
down her thighs; the people below are wet

with stolen light.
        No umbrellas
strew their colors—it's too hard

for that—but dogs quiver under lumber
busses splash the same
sloppy syllable across each sidewalk,
the metro opens its mouth, the balcony

becomes a cup.
        The faucet won't turn off. The soap,
the soap has fallen and her body, slick

is shining.
        Draghitza shakes some water
drops from her fingertips, she blurs

in latent steam, is lost in surfeit
sharpens and blurs again.

She has fingerprints and large hands.
She tastes slightly of metal and of sea.

She is always smaller in person
than we expect and more
        than we remember.

CASTRIES

A City's Death By Fire

By Derek Walcott

After that hot gospeller has levelled all but the churched sky,
I wrote the tale by tallow of a city's death by fire;
Under a candle's eye, that smoked in tears, I
Wanted to tell, in more than wax, of faiths that were snapped like wire.
All day I walked abroad among the rubbled tales,
Shocked at each wall that stood on the street like a liar;
Loud was the bird-rocked sky, and all the clouds were bales
Torn open by looting, and white, in spite of the fire.
By the smoking sea, where Christ walked, I asked, why
Should a man wax tears, when his wooden world fails?
In town, leaves were paper, but the hills were a flock of faiths;
To a boy who walked all day, each leaf was a green breath
Rebuilding a love I thought was dead as nails,
Blessing the death and the baptism by fire.

CASTRIES

An Offering

By Vladimir Lucien

for Derek Walcott

Give me the city any day
from high up on Mt. Pleasant under the *Pòwiyé*
tree; from Government House where I will see
lights crawl up Barnard Hill, speckling
the curved harbor. Let it unfurl, map-like;
something whose life is still being planned
something we can admit our mistakes in making
something we can tear up, crumple and begin again.
Give it to me from quiet Vigie, from the lighthouse
or in Careille; a Château in Upper La Pansee. Is it bad
that I want the city, like a lover, at certain times?
Over cocoa tea or with the smell of Bonnie's bread making a
violin of my nose;
when it gurgles, early morning, in a pigeon's mouth;
that I want the city when and where I want it?
Like on abandoned streets that remember
the fire: Short Street, Queen Street, Prince Alfred's Basin
or in the small pseudo-Italian restaurant just off the Boulevard;
on any of its surrounding hills where you can truly see it—
make it fill the eye the way true tears do. Give it to me when it
rains and we shelter under the verandahs of old Colonial houses.
Give me Jeremie Street at midnight, rinsed clean of rummies
and the clatter of dominoes, without its heaps of produce and
vendors: dark, unpeopled and navigable. Straight. Unequivocal.
Give me to the city on a bright afternoon, whenever the
ambulance must soften traffic for me, jolting the languid necks of
idlers; when the hearse slow-dancing with eyes, must leave
the Cathedral heading to the crowded cemetery at Choc.

GEORGETOWN

Georgetown

By Mark McWatt

Georgetowns of my memory flee
from me now, taking with them
those long-lost houses, whose quiet corners
and dark, hiding cupboards used to sing
songs of comfort and belonging
to a country-boy come to town to see
whether a city and its hallowed schools
can compensate for river-islands
and dark creeks, haunted by blue
butterflies; and all that wild, incomparable space
a childish heart had learnt to love...

And Georgetown outdid my expectations,
with the grid-patterned rhythm
of its eagerly-cycled streets and the free-
verse of its traffic noises, borne
on fresh sea-wall breeze; and the litany
of teachers' names, and two cathedrals
pointing straight to heaven, and an
unexpected bounty of cousins
and other relatives, and lovely wooden buildings,
so perfectly maintained...

And schoolboys were taught
how to discern in all of this
the colonial noose around their city's
—their country's, their own—neck,
and to long for freedom...

But freedom is a funny game;

citizens fled as Independence came;
'Fear of another Cuba' is the least
offensive name one could give
to the reason for the interference
of fat, self-righteous western powers
that doomed this country and city of ours
to fifty years of misery and corruption...

Georgetown shrugged and settled
Into a shabbier version of itself,
learning to live with faded paint
and rotting wood and canals choked
with garbage. Everyone knows now
that political parties and their minions
are more important than capital cities...

And yet, if one ignores the filth
and the concrete monsters
and the flash of laundered money,
one must still love a city that fed
the soul of a schoolboy—and can still tug at his heart
like the string of a far, faded kite
riding high on the sea-wall breeze,
this and every Easter Monday.

GUATEMALA CITY

Guatemala City: A Roadkill

By Alan Mills

This quiet animal
looks a bit like me, in its
pool of blood,
almost floating in red, it has
something of me in it.
This animal that's been crushed,
that's been given it hard,
and no longer knows if it's dog or chicken
or plain martyr or what.
It's silence speaks only to asphalt,
to those eyes that see it while doing nothing;
to those who vomit when they see it.
Something is here,
something of my brightness
in each particle that's pummeled
by passing wheels.

—*Translation from the Spanish by* Andrew O'Donnell

HAVANA

Searching for an Unemployed Lover

By Pedro Pérez Sarduy

Havana lives on the edge of darkness
with its air contaminated by tourists
and uncommon dissidents
where the young offer of a dress tightly fitting
the circumstances of the latest fashion trots ironically
along the sea front
among seemingly exotic cocktails
and the perennial indifference of a commissar
also confused when it comes to persuasion.

Whatever form it took
Havana was there mine and more sensual than usual
leaning out as always from her balconies
gazing tirelessly towards the sea of girls and boys of the past
dressed in lycra and the reflection of a forbidden disco
with that dizzy silhouette
facing a pale face unexpected and unknown
wearing foreign clothes, of course.

However
there is no time to lose for the poor beggar
searching for the right moment for a quick feel
and the game between tongues.
After all
we are in the presence of an age tormented by so many
ailments.

There is no time to lose either
because tomorrow afternoon would already be tonight
and also another peaceful dawn

rewarded with a sumptuous supper or simply a supper
with no imported frills
for as long as the reign of austerity lasts
or just a daring invitation.

In these times only *okana*
the solitary African conch who predicts ill omens
restlessly roams the earth thirsting for so many kind acts
wasted
incoherent offerings and sullied pleas
something is wanting in the look
like that aimed at assisting the needy
so much that today Monday seems to exude a certain arrogance
which was never entirely rational.

What joy if you were with me now
O mío Queen of the Sea
You who dare to ride the waves mounted on Taurus
among precious turquoise gems which adorn gentle crown
You who always ignore the secretly agreed cry of the initiate
before dusk and you keep going in my arms
accompanied only by the sound of dry coconuts
which have always been dry.
You did not return from the grand feast
and were speaking with yourself
endeavouring to satisfy the freshness of honey
on the tips of yours breasts
your body writhing fresh with clean waters
penetrating the most intimate point of your night
there where shame halts frightened.

And before parting all the shadows
were innocent and silently similar.

—*Translated by* Jean Stubbs

KINGSTON

New Kingston
By Colin Channer

Poolside. Summer. Sixties-style hotel. Blocky cut-out
of the modern in a thought-out business zone.

New Kingston. Far from slum and harbor.
Second take on commerce set up midway to the hills.
Far from court, wholesale and prison.
Far from market where the black goat
gets skinned out in public,
cutlassed for the curry and the drum.

This poolside scene could stand for California,
deals being cut at café tables, sharp sunglasses,
white skin on tinting brown. And, lined along
the chaises: potted ficus, cacti, palms.

Downtown, which could play New Orleans
in a movie, lean trees that keep secrets,
ancient confidantes of slaves,
human beings who willed their lives to pollen,
said, 'Take it' as the atlas caught the noose.

On certain evenings, after sunset,
grains of hazing yellow crack and *duppies* saunter out,
float-linger on the stench of progress:
diesel, warm garbage, potholes dredged with filth,
cast-off people filming with a brutal human funk.

When these grains explode inhaling stutters,
eyes and nostrils run—yes, this does occur—
and centuries and centuries of loss come back as odors,

memos from the limbic, scents of what the outpost
ranked as vital, needed, vetted,
listed, ordered, planned for, brokered,
lashed below for months of voyage:
burlap, buck shot, barrels; powder, niggers, cod.

In a tinny speaker in a mango tree some reggae natters.
The tree is big and afro-ed, strapping with white washing on its trunk.
But fruitless. What species? Tom the Wrinkly Barman doesn't know.
Quips it's barren as he shakes a dry martini. Thing hasn't borne
in fifty years. A ruckus takes a branch.

KINGSTON

Impossible Flying

'Palms of Victory/ Deliverance is here!'

1980 Jamaica Labour Party campaign song

By Kwame Dawes

1
On Kingston's flat worn earth,
everything is hard as glass.
The sun smashes into the city – no breath,
no wind, just the engulfing, asthmatic noonday.

We move with the slow preservation
of people saving their strength
for a harsher time. 1980:
this land has bled – so many betrayals –
and the indiscriminate blooding of hope
has left us quivering, pale,
void, the collapsed possibilities
causing us to limp. We are a country
on the edge of the manic euphoria
of a new decade: Reagan's nodding
grin ripples across the basin's
surface. We dare to dream
that in the spin and tongues of Kapo
perhaps we too will fly this time,
will lift ourselves from the slough
of that dream-maker's decade –
the '70s when we learned things only
before suspected: our capacity for blood,
our ability to walk through a shattered
city, picking our routine way to work
each morning. We are so used now to the ruins,
perhaps more than that, perhaps to wearing

our sackcloth and ash as signs of our
hope, the vanity of survival.

In that decade when a locksman
could prance the streets with a silver
magic trail in his wake, how we fought
to be poor, to be sufferers, to say
Looking at you the better one; how
we cultivated our burden-bearing,
white-squall, hungry belly,
burlap-wearing, Cariba-suited
socialist dream; how reggae
with its staple of faith, fame
and fortune spoke its revelation
from the speakers of souped-up
BMWs. Gone now, all gone.

We have thrown off that dead skin now;
and the fleets of squat Ladas
are rusting, O Havana.
We've grown too cynical for such austerity
or perhaps we did not suffer enough.
So on such blank and startled days, we dream
of flight. How we hope: *Dance!*
Dance, damn it! Dance, damn it! Be happy!
Our apocalypse echoes on the sound system
and we dance. These laws, these new laws,
these palm leaves, these clamouring bells,
so desperate for deliverance,
this insipid green in the future, and we all
stare at the unflinching sky
and will our hearts to fly.

2
And how you ran, sprinting
down Carlisle Avenue,
your face set against the bare wind;

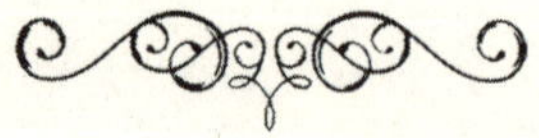

you were spreading your arms
undulating in complete faith
in the wind's lift,

the physics of the updraft;
past the low fences,
the skittish yelping dogs,

the streaks of telephone wires,
the hibiscus hedges
a blur of green and pink

and smudged off-white;
and me calling you,
trying hard to bring you back;

me catching up,
behind you now, our heat,
our panting, the slap of bare feet

on the soft asphalt;
and I reached for you,
held you by the waist,

drawing you down;
and it felt in that instant
not like a shattering of faith

but a struggle to keep
you home, for each tendon
of your body throbbed

with the lightness of a body
prepared for flight.
And my betrayal was to become

the burden,
the anchor you had
for years longed to shake off.

Stillness, the gaping crowd
staring at this sudden accident:
two men in a heap

of twisted limbs
on the road;
you saying, *This time, this time,*

this time if you had let me,
it would have happened.
I too felt the vanity

of our beaching.
The bells shimmered;
the dispatches were in:

No one
was flying
no more.

KINGSTOWN

Flotsam and Jetsam

By Philip Nanton

It's just nature, we say
this tsunami of empire that washed us up here.

> ***Final offer gentlemen. Five pounds three shillings***
> ***for the seasoned buck.***

When that last wave rolled back it exposed a humble butter fish
twitching, flipping and flapping, worn down town

> ***Five dollar for that heap?***
> ***Ground provisions no longer cheap.***

its mouth opening and closing

> ***you'd be amazed what deals can be struck with care***
> ***in our little colony's market square***

sucking its death of sea air wondering why its fins
fail to glide through water while its scales
slap the keel of some hard-hulled fishing boat.

> ***Only thirty dollar Mother Lynch. Ah beg yuh.***
> ***Mammy sending money for the wear and tear***

When did we become indifferent to the hucksters
with their tight grip on the sidewalks

> ***DRIVER! Why you can't look where you coming?***

their five shoe boxes, twenty-three combs and
white trestle tables that groan with out-size brassieres?

> ***Rasta! Why YOU can't go where you looking?***

We're cool with the pool of smart boys skulking in Middle Street
each with his three card stool waiting to fool the next passer-by

You and your family........ think they big-shot.

while Sam solicits donations for his phantom football teams.

It have a funeral at four o'clock sharp.

Who turns a hair when Bazodie marches through Market Square
wearing buttoned down wrists, short pants, head swathed in a
balaclava.

I wonder why people always have to die 'pon a
week-day.

With his termite ridden piece of treated pine he executes a
perfect off drive
and follows it through okras and eddoes in the firm belief that he
is Brian Lara.

He? He say he going to come back.

And we look away when the rain fills the drains

Who want to go to Hell can go to Hell.

and cockroaches thick as locusts swim out of the open gutters
like recently hatched leather-backs lost on their way to sea.

You are the shepherd, they are the flock

But all's not lost. The wharf sign welcomes everyone
to a capital city proclaiming itself a hive of industry.

Boy, don't wear jeans and tee shirt again
when you come to see me.
They keep you too hot.

LA PAZ

Poem for La Paz

By Carlos D. Mesa Gisbert

I look at you
Horizon dark with smoke and melancholy
I remember the sounds of your nights
That stay with me
Collar turned up
Pure starless black
Wind tangled on the corners
I imagine the diamond that you are in my hands
My fingers trace the paths that arrive at your doors
I wait for the moment of entering you again
First softly
To the center of your inclement rains
To drench myself
Then with the passion of an attacker
What magic do your blue corners hold
Relatives of space?
I will never forget
My footprints in your heart
Or the three silhouettes of snow
That hypnotize my senses
I have walked you so often
That I stayed with you
In the memory of men
Exhausted from making you
How strange the spell that calls me
City born of war
Which floods my minutes with desire for you
Lips dry without your valley
Behind the high plateau
Scattered
As if falling

You wait for me
Because you always wait for the bodies of your body
Because you know that death becomes a friend
Beneath your hills

—*Translated from the Spanish by* David Shook

LIMA

The Recycle City (on these days)

By Victoria Guerrero

With the heart torn apart I walk through the bridge
a metallic surface unable to decay
down
an enormous river flows
        icy
A beautiful blue mirror shelters their dead
three punks
a university professor
an unknown woman (always we are)
flow over its water

I call them my post-modern Ophelias in the Recycle City
do not recycling is illegal- said the landlady
and immediately I began to remove the splinters of my heart

No one would say that those bodies attract me
nevertheless
part of me goes to that side
where we see the emptiness as a memory of a happy childhood
        the waters expect for me
        and I fail

I pull on the other side
no less uncertain
where the lights of the cars swallow each other
        each other
        each other
and my body would be swallowed by them
        a nudity of horror
        I said to me

and again
I fail

Across the bridge (the beginning or the end never mind)
a brightness river flows under my feet
Rímac River rises over my memory as it is:
a dark river bed that shadows our misery
nevertheless
this hostile muddy river bed perhaps once was good
and with its tender claws cradled
my grandparents
my father
my mother
my sister
little luz maría
or me

sudaca whose shadow is reflected in a beautiful pale river
willing to be broken by the first touch of light
or by the scream of another body (the splash of death)
as all of these
injured by innocence
in the recycle city
whose bridges never collapse

— *Translated by* Enrique Bernales

LIMA

Lima

By Abhay K.

When sun rays fall on colonial facades,
the Inca temples and pre-Columbian ruins
along the Costa Verde
let's climb the crumbling cliffs
then descend down the Malecon
to surf the waves of the Pacific

let's listen to solemn chants of Peru
and its sublime poetry
or submerge into its history
let's meet at the Museo Larco,
Chimú, Chancay, Chincha,
Nazca and Inca

let's cross the bridge of sighs in Barranco
and go to crowded nightclubs
to dance to the tropical beats
and when we get tired
and we will, let's find our way
through Lima's messy streets

let's go to Puruchuco
all tied up in ropes—head to toe
and lie with a mummy
and then to Pachacamac
to bow to the Earth Maker
to climb the pyramids

then let's head to the love park
to smell the rose blooming in the desert

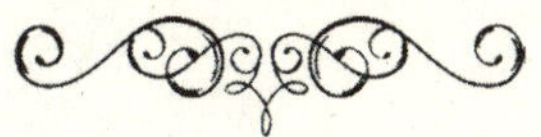

and look at the Lima Bay
let's climb the Huaca Pucllana
and taste Chicha Morada and Pisco sour
on banks of the river Rimac

let's enter the abode of last Inca on the San Cristobal Hill
get inside Lima's old train station—a time machine
and see it metamorphose into an extraordinary thing
let's look at intricately carved wooden balconies
at the Plaza de Armas and steal a glimpse
of the Gran Hotel Bolivar at the San Martin

let's see the masked dancers dancing *Chonquinada*
and pigeons hovering over the San Francisco cathedral—
the flying spirits of those buried underneath in the labyrinth
of catacombs, and then let's go to Larcomar
to watch the sun set over the Pacific, and to end it all
let our spirit soar with a thousand fountains at the aqua park.

MANAGUA

Managua 6:30 P.M.

By Ernesto Cardenal

In the evening the neon lights are soft
and the mercury streetlamps, pale and beautiful …
And the red star on a radio tower
in the twilight sky of Managua
looks as pretty as Venus
and an ESSO sign looks like the moon

The red taillights of the cars are mystical

(The soul is like a girl kissed hard behind a car)
TACA BUNGE KLM SINGER
MENNEN HTM GÓMEZ NORGE
RPM SAF ÓPTICA SELECTA
all proclaim the glory of God!
(Kiss me under the glowing signs oh God)
KODAK TROPICAL RADIO F&C REYES
they spell your Name
in many colors.
            'They broadcast
            the news …'
I don't know
what else they mean
I don't defend the cruelty behind these lights
And if I have to give a testimony about my times
it's this: They were primitive and barbaric
but poetic

—*Translated from the Spanish by* Jonathan Cohen

MEXICO CITY

Space-Time

By Zoë Brigley

Here is an island like a jewel or scarab
on the flat lagoon where herons wade.
They walk the circling zócalo from city door
to city gate and find that every pathway
leads to the water where birds wing air-currents:
paths of filings in iron magnetism.

A buzzard of the Mexican highlands is drawn
by feeding grounds of turtle, shrimp and beetle:
gods that fell headlong from the sun's ripening course
to merge with the earthbound souls of the dead
and plague them invisibly for life and vigour,
the buzz of regret eclipsing the Milky Way.

She shows him the stars of the southern hemisphere
Here, the beekeeper wooing the hives with his charms,
and here, a lady—Obsidian Butterfly
spelled with stars, throwing arrows against tidal winds.
No more of the past, that which has always happened,
a remote island that jolts to life each day.

Lying on the dock, she puts an eye to the slats:
the lake's quiet pulse of bird foot or paddle
teaches her to hear and know a bird arced in space,
a pebble thrown up over water in the dark.
The sky will persist for a thousand years and I
will remain here young, in search of the Southern Cross.

MONTEVIDEO

Austral Tongue

By Luis Bravo

1.

There is a watery light in the pub, the veins of the gray marble hold a small glass with grappa that shall bite the throat. Memory shall shuffle its cards over a counter of time and time.

2.

I return through the street of childhood. It's identical to the scent of the Indian Lilac trees.

I enter into its chess tiles and everything fits: pieces of houses, the eyes of the trees, two sparrows resting on the lamp posts. Everything imitates the memories I have of these and other things, like pieces of heaven. I believe that if I stop recalling this street, the whole city would disappear from East to West on the bay of visions.

3.

They would call it *la coquette* forever gazing at its reflection on each side of the Sea.

Montevideo, a girl like my mother, perched on the roofs of *Isla de Flores Street*; hidden in the midst of the vines of her neighbor *Don Paco Espínola*, who is writing the first fictionalized shadows about the virgin city.

4.

'Montevideo in green and blue' imagines the painter, staining gaps of azure between the leafy crown of the *Ombú*. On the vigil for the Negro, *Dr. Figari* saw a *candombe* in colors.

The Negroes had given three drums to the night, *borocotó chás chás, borocotó chás chás, borocotó* rattles the words of Ildefonso, white poet of Negritude.

5.
Green trees, naked spiral of the city, always tall lookouts.
At the *Parque Rivera* I discovered the flavor of long kisses, invisible to the worldly noise.
On the bark of time the lovers inscribe secrets that weave destinies.
And so on.

6.
The North Wind is suffocating like a Turkish bath.
The *Pampero* riding from the South bursts in the city, untamed colt on the silver wake of the River.

Bruno Mauricio, of Biscay from the suburb of *Zabala*, took years to found San Felipe and Santiago of Montevideo. Each time the sailboat crossed from Buenos Aires, the Southeastern Wind would disarray his curly French wig.

7.
In the squall a magical voice is heard singing tangos over the rocks of *La Mulata* beach. That man, well combed, arms outstretched to the horizon, croons melodies that cradles the wide river.
In tailcoat, back turned to the city, on the wall of *Cubo del Sur*, young Isidore Ducasse says:

'oh! ancient ocean...a prolonged breath of sadness that sounds like the murmur of a soft breeze, passes by, leaving indelible tracks...'

Reclined on the bunk of the *Hotel Pyramides* the fierce eye of a French cursed poet invites him with a pipe of sweet Cannabis. Feverish sheets soiled with blood of octopus fall at Lautréamont feet, staining estuary waters.
The thunder of drums beats in synch with the heart.
The folds of the Band Union from the Negro José Santa Cruz dream a bandoneon after the battle.
The polyphonic *clarinada* of the neighborhoods climbs the stage of painted faces.

Getting down *Cuareim Street* sounds the Yoruba tam tam of a goddess. On her way lights candles over the waves of *Playa Ramirez*, baroque cathedral of sand altars.
The howling stave of austral tongues is Montevideo.

8.
False portal to the Citadel where another Time remains open at the back of *Sarandí* Street, name of an unlikely battle in which J. L. Borges fights under the open sky, oriental dagger in hand.

9.
Whether the Florentine Américo Vespucci in 1501, or De Albo, Greek pilot for the Portuguese Fernando de Magalhães, in 1520, no one knows for certain who arrived first to this mount, nor where your name comes from, mysterious Montevideo.
Who in the mirror of your waters sees its reflection and pronounces your name, shall never forget you, Montevideo.

10.
'Oracle of hell', called the first Jesuits the yerba mate Guaraní. To drink mate is the perdition of *Montevideanos*. Not thanks to God, but to *Caá Yarí*.

11.
Haunt of artists, staging of the great theater of the world whose spectators celebrate always with discreet charm. (Except for the popular glories in the art of football).

12.
This is not a city for tourists but for explorers of the spirit: 'the Montevideo spoken of is not the real Montevideo'.

13.
In Montevideo the poets dream a dream within a dream. This is why they are known as Orientals.

—*Translated by* Laura Haiek, *assisted by* L. Bravo

NASSAU

Nassau Circa Christmas Time

By Lelawatee Manoo-Rahming

Junkanoo impersonations
the city invents and erases them

ink slips off fringed newspapers
and rushes like the wind

from a cold front
reinventing itself into words

percussive, frenzied
African apparitions

caught in the spectrum of night
colours flashing red gold purple

a cowfoot glimmers
in the hem of skirt

as the painted lady swirls
La Diablesse stalking the streets

of erased bugle sounds
ghosts of poodles yapping on broken balconies

La Diablesse searching for le lagahoo
half-man, half-beast

lashing his chains in the stickfight

in the split of time
Africa circa 1808 explodes

on Bay Street circa 2008
a rushing whistling wind tribe

following the beat and scent of blood
nous ne sommes pas morts... nous ne sommes pas morts
we are not dead... we are not dead

NEW YORK

Photographs of Old New York

By Alfred Corn

They stare back into an increate future,
Dead stars, burning still. Air how choked with soot
One breathed then, the smudged grays and blacks impressed
In circles around East European eyes,
Top hats, a brougham, the laundry that hung
Like crowds of ghosts over common courtyards.
Dignity still knew how to thrust its hand
Into a waistcoat, bread plaited into shapes
How to dress a window, light under the El
Fall as negative to cast-iron shadows.
Assemble Liberty plate by plate—so
This giant dismembered arm still emerges
From folds of bronze and floats over the heads
Of bearded workmen riveted in place
By an explosion of magnesium they've learned
To endure. Then, Union. Rally. March. Strike.

And still the wretched refugees swarming
Out from Ellis Island, the glittering door,
To prosper or perish. Or both...The men
Don't see the women; or see how deftly hems
Can be lifted at curbs—well, any eye would
Be caught by that tilt of hat, profile, bearing.
Others strive to have mattered too, stolid
Forms that blush and crouch over sewing machines,
Haunt the libraries, speak on platforms.
Did they? And did this woman, who clearly still
Speaks no English, her head scarf, say, Russian?
A son stands at her side, crop-haired, in clumpy
Shoes. She stares straight forward, reserved, aware,

Embattled. The deep-set eyes say something
About the emptiness of most wishes; and
About her hopes. She knows the odds are poor.
Or, the odds are zero, counted from here.
The past survives its population
And is unkind. Triumph no more than failure
In the longest run ever fails to fail.
Is that the argument against shuffling,
Dealing, and reshuffling these photographs?
They are not mementos of death alone,
But of life lived variously, avatars
Energy, insight, cruelty took—and love.
Variousness: the great kaleidoscope
Of time, its snowflake pictures, form after
Form, collapsing into the future, hours,
Days, seasons, generations that rise up
And fall like leaves, each one a hand inscribed
With the fragile calligraphy of selfhood;
The human fate given a human face.

NEW YORK

Phone Booth (New York, 1988)

By Annette Hagemann

After Helen Levitt's photograph of the same name

Puerto Rico that was nice
the old homelike heat
here in the north you just get it
through the body of the mother
who stands here with her black coiffured curls
a blue and beige floral dress and the shape
of a vase: narrow at the top and at the ankles,
in between much room for flower water and rum,
Puerto Rican cooking skills, unborn children
and from the outside leaning against her
several born ones in various (small) sizes
none of them leaving the clan: not even
when she enters the phone booth

—*Translated from German by* Anatoly Kudryavitsky and Yulia Kudryavitskaya

OTTAWA

Ottawa Simple

By Francoise Roy

You, the princely gal, the meek one,
the almost invisible lady one hardly talks about,
are no stone Cinderella
like those ancient cities
who sleep aloof on their treasure chests —
(I think, for instance, of the skeleton
of the lost Tenochtitlan
battered five hundred years ago
like a wingless bird tossed in supranatural winds).
I wonder if you still dream
of the maple forest that used to grow where you now stand,
if you still remember your gown of greenery
or the endless tree cathedral
where a flock of Natives
glided over long-lost lakes like weightless insects
performing a nuptial dance.
No gold ever glistened where you were born,
no buried pyramid blinks an eye at you
like a sweet ghost in a nightmare.
The horses of the newcomers
were not an army of live scarecrows like further south,
but the animate pieces of an orderly chess game
claiming a piece of land to build a parliament,
a grid of demure streets, the Rideau canal
and tidy tulip flowerbeds.
The only thing you, the snow-white princess
who lacks the maddening glamour of others,
have kept as a token of a past
where only snow altered the course of time
is your Algonquin name, *adawe.*

OTTAWA

On Ottawa

By Scott Alain

when I die
bury me
in Ottawa

because Parliament Hill
is a Gothic-bricked
phoenix

and for over 180 years
the Rideau Canal
has connected neighbors
with the sprawl of its capillaries
[by canoe in the summer
and ice-skate blades in the cold]

gone is the name 'Bytown'
gone are the lumber yards
and gone are the riots

yet that immutable dream
of a community
built along the Kichisippi
hangs proudly
in the imaginings
of its inhabitants

because in our city
everybody arrives an immigrant
but becomes a component
of its flourishing character

like a mound of fallen red-maple foliage
or
the globed lamps lining the wáter

PANAMA CITY

While You are Sleeping

By Lucy Cristina Chau

While you are sleeping
a new building is growing in the corner
and all the waged elves who build it
burn their words on fire
to give themselves a little relief.
On the next street
the red, green and yellow lights play with the time
throwing cars to each other
and organizing a deviled claxons orchestra
– without music score – working as a soundtrack
for the opera of the collective indifference.
But just beside you
– while you're sleeping –
a woman is drawing herself
using the precise lines of the infinite
and preparing – as in an invented ritual –
the clandestine meeting
with your kisses.

PARAMARIBO

Paramaribo

By Abhay K.

Alonso, Juan, Amerigo — the voyagers rushed
to the Wild Coast in search of an Inca El Dorado

instead they discovered Parmurbo—
a village inhabited by the Indians

and when the tobacco and sugar plantations declined
a mighty city arose on the banks of the river Suriname

now, Wilhelmina— the displaced Dutch queen
looks at Goslar— a sunken ghost ship, from a rusty island.

PORT-AU-PRINCE

Port-au-Prince

By Denize Lauture

Port-au-Prince
Pronouncing your first syllable
I bit my tongue's right side
Pronouncing your second syllable
I bit my tongue 's left side
On your third syllable
My teeth almost severed my tongue's tip
Bloody is the spit in my mouth
Like the sea-waters in your bay
My lips drip, drip blood
Like your crumbled walls

Port-au-Prince
Conceived during a violent eruption
Grew up to become a pretty woman
With luscious lips
Moons and suns, each passing year
Illuminated widening of your hip
Explosion of your breasts
And your enchanted meadow
Bore numerous children

But neither children nor priests
Neither pirates nor kings or gods
For whom you erect flowery altars
Serve you paradisiacal food
Thunder your Rada and Asotor drums
And become entranced
Sprinkle blessed water
To drive away the evil

Left by the first cross
Erected on Ayiti Toma's shore

Many bards and poets sang of
Your golden days that would return
Rows of laurel trees would rise again
And cast their pink and white petals in your streets
Tall palm trees shall sway again
With their giant leaves during kinder winds
And aim their green arrows to the blue sky
Mahogany trees and *Kita Nago*
Shall grow stronger roots, limbs and leaves
And help you withstand the fiercest hurricanes
And the deadliest earthquakes
Two eternal progress lamps will ever shine
Atop Fort National and Hospital Mountain.

Rada, Asotor	Names of two special Vodou drums
Ayiti Toma	Affectionate name Haitians use to refer to Haiti
Kita Nago	Name of a huge symbolic mahogany cross carried by relaying men across the country
Hospital Mountain	A tall mountain hovering above Port-au-Prince
Fort National	A fort built during colonial time above a hill to defend the city

PORT OF SPAIN

Night in the Gardens of Port of Spain

By Derek Walcott

Night, the black summer, simplifies her smells
into a village; she assumes the impenetrable

musk of the negro, grows secret as sweat,
her alleys odorous with shucked oyster shells,

coals of gold oranges, braziers of melon.
Commerce and tambourines increase her heat.

Hellfire or the whorehouse: crossing Park Street,
a surf of sailor's faces crest, is gone

with the sea's phosphoresence; the boites-de-nuit
tinkle like fireflies in her thick hair.

Blinded by headlamps, deaf to taxi klaxons,
she lifts her face from the cheap, pitch oil flare

toward white stars, like cities, flashing neon,
burning to be the bitch she must become.

As daylight breaks the coolie turns his tumbril
of hacked, beheaded coconuts towards home.

PORT OF SPAIN

Portraits of Port-of-Spain

By Lauren K. Alleyne

1.
Mummy is a town girl through and through,
so plenty weekends we would 'make a run'
to Port-of-Spain. Each visit was a lesson—
from the time we jump out of the taxi
on Independence Square. The first stop
was the Cathedral, ancient and grand
with its spires and pipe organ. Quick prayers,
then, the streets in order of importance:
Fredrick Street, the main artery of the city's
throb and chaos, a thoroughfare of commerce,
from Woolworth's (now Excellent Stores);
to the rasta men selling hand-crafted leather
sandals and knitted hats in red, green, and gold;
to the dark glass doorways that opened
into entire worlds of delicious and glittering
things—dhal pies in Golden Gate Mall;
electronics stores booming with sound,
cousin Judy's trendy clothes shop. Last
stop was Maraj Jewelers where mummy liked
to *take a peek* at the glowing glass cases.
Queen Street was for cloth stores—
Jimmy Aboud's, Moses', and Mansoor's,
where we fingered bolt after bolt of fabric
for church dresses, white polyester for school
shirts, tetrex for uniforms, and at Christmas time,
curtains for every room of the house.
Charlotte Street held all the bargains—
cheap market bags and knickknacks,

but more important to us, the *Chinee* shops
where endless varieties of *salt prunes,*
preserved plums, and *red mango*,
could be found in mouthwatering abundance.
Ladies of the night, lived on George Street,
Mummy warned, and we never turned
down that corner. There was nothing fun
on St. Vincent or Edward or Pembroke,
or Abercomby Streets, but still we learned
their names, pointed them out one by one
until they rolled off our tongues with ease,
until they felt like ours.

2.
In social studies we learn the Queen's
Park Savannah is the largest roundabout
in the world, but for us it is a playground
to run in what seems like endless grass
until we are wet with sweat. We can play
catch, and *red light, green light, 1-2-3,*fly
Christmas kites, ride our bicycles, and
never hit a wall or a fence. When we are tired,
we can watch the men cutting coconuts
into chalices with two chops of their cutlasses,
or the fellas making footballs fly into nets.
Mummy calls us over to the *snow cone* man
she thinks is cleanest—she's been looking
to see who picks his nose or scratches
his privates without washing his hands—
and we line up. First the conical cup,
then the *shave ice,* then the glorious
syrups, thick and sweet red, orange,
blue and green, with condensed milk
drizzled on top for good measure—
the whole rainbow in our little fists,
our hungry mouths sucking it in.

3.
The University of Woodford Square
scares me as a child—vagrants sleeping
on the benches, toothless men and women
with lottery tickets strung on board
and wire—them looking too tired to
even try to sell you the dream.
Mummy tells me back in the day,
this was the place to be, with your afro
and dashiki, to hear people talk
about *black power* and *black people.*
She shakes her head and humphs
as we hustle through to get to the red house.
We never linger there with the madmen
and the ghosts.

4.
Is carnival and I am in the center of the action—
Bam! —in the middle of Port-of Spain.
Mummy's home, and I am with her friend
Ann Marie, who is both older than I
and younger than Mummy enough to be cool.
We *chipping* with the bands, the crowds
pressing against us like a hot sigh. Carnival,
let me tell you, is like nothing you've seen
unless you've seen it—a festival of bodies
on the move, song and sun like a benediction,
the air waves sing to a beat which takes the whole year
to let it go. And truth, this is the closest I have been
to the *bacchanal*, so I give myself over to it.
When I look up, look around, Ann Marie is gone.
Every face is unfamiliar, covered in paint, glitter,
and glee, and I can't see anything but faces.
Not a street sign in sight, the city swallowed
by the locust revelers. The surge of panic is true,
but momentary. Then an exhale of triumph.

This is what I know: behind me is Independence
Square, and the big stage is right on the savannah.
My mother didn't make no *country bookie*—
this is Port-of-Spain: I can find my way anywhere.

QUITO

Postcard of Downtown Quito with Me in the Midst of It

By Edwin Madrid

Mountains break through the night sky, insane streets that go up and down, bells ringing, more bells, cars skid as they turn the corners, young men head toward the discotheques kicking beer cans, couples kiss while the traffic lights change. Music escapes from between the legs of a miniskirt and the obscene heels of a boy who takes his first steps in the real world. Fantasy chicks get lost above the sound of squeaking brakes and roaring car engines.
And there I go, barely able to stop myself, embraced by a woman like a flag that waves to me, through the bars and seedy hotels.

ROSEAU

A Stray (astray) in Roseau

By Delroy Nesta Williams

How do you walk through Roseau
And not smell the stench
Three, four 'paros' taking a hit
Behind the broken down wooden fence
Crouched over without a concern
Withering away into obscurity
While young children look down from their porches
Point fingers, laugh and make jokes
But this 'paro' man wanted a future
Just like the one you hope for
River Street, Cork Street and even Virgin Lane
The streets of the city are all stained
Roseau has gone to the dogs
And who is to be blamed?
With a hand out they ask for a dollar
Harassing you on every street corner
But the pungent smell is a turn off
So you hold your nose and show no love
What you do to the least of your brothers?
No one seems to bother
And we carry on our merry way
Unless we need a favor
Something we don't want to pay for the full price for
So instead we hire the 'paro' labour
But a cost deferred is still a price to pay, someday
So while you show no love
You walk the city streets going to the Cathedral
So routine that you see almost nothing
In your Sunday best and two-edged sword
It's funny how you carry the good Book but ignore the words

Along your journey to cast empty prayers to the Lord above
The rhetoric of last Sunday becomes the gospel retold today
Ignoring that the 'paro' problem is a situation
That you've created when you turn a blind eye
And instead cast judgment
But the 'paro' was once just a passer by
Yes, that could just be you
In a few years after being knocked down
By a society that creates problems
And offers little or no solutions
And so Roseau rest afloat
On a cloud of issues
But the least of which we see
Is the 'paro' roaming the city streets!

**A paro is local dialect/créole for a drug user or drug addict.*

SAN JOSE

The Others
By Luis Chaves

San Jose was nothing but
some lights in the distance:
a bureaucratic constellation
looking a little less underdeveloped in the dark.

Everything else, empty cans of beer
too warm to have liked the taste of;
the barely-lit bulb
of a car with the doors open;
an emotion that, deflated
we call fondness.

—*Translation by* Andrea Mickus

SAN SALVADOR

San Salvador

By Abhay K.

Between a lake and a volcano
at an abandoned site
of the Nahuat nation
is a city at the coast
of the Pacific ocean.

There in a blue and yellow checked dome
rests Archbishop Oscar A. Romero

Nearby the plaza Gerardo Barrios
remembers that historic day – the day
the Chapultepec accords were signed
ending the twenty-two years of civil war
and scores of people had flooded the city square.

SANTIAGO

Chronicle of Santiago

By Veronica Zondek

He prowls.
His eye scans the Santiago Valley.
He feels the homemade tepidity.
Beneath a cloud and above the snow
hangs a ghost.
His word leaves no sky for appeal.

In this valley
pregnancy is a circumstance.
Life is weird
and stretches out as a statistic.
Death hides away behind thick walls
in a black disposable bag.

Numbers do their job.
Progress kills all attempts at recollection
and buries deep belonging's cry.
Memory is not desire.
Domesticated parks grow.

A train flaps by across a subterranean valley.
The field is populated with houses of recycled cardboard.
Logic is challenged.
The woods along the riverside are cut down.
Hormones are sown.
Boasts are made.

Security is heightened.
The approach of disaster is foretold.
Impunity is voted for.

Consensus is encouraged.
They fumigate the polluted one with the evil eye:
whoever is not dressed in grey or navy blue
whoever looks to the other side.
The animal is locked up for its wildness.
The national anthem is sung out loud.

SANTO DOMINGO

The City of Screams

By Jael Uribe

Happy people run wild
in the streets of Santo *Domingo*
—the city of screams

shadows dance on concrete
this city has a contemplating eye
buildings tremble mysteriously

graffiti
on the red brick roads
all over *El Conde*

Taínos' souls— the ghosts
of the Caribbean walk around
seeking redemption

sand-steps melt in water
of Boca Chica's beach
embraced by an ocean no one sees

at the night on February 27
police sirens fill the streets
in the carnival the whole city parties

ringing bells of *Diablos Cojuelos*
playing merengue
enacting colourful parody of the evil

people dance on the asphalt
make love
to the Dominican glory.

El Conde	A famous street on Colonial Zone at the historical center of Santo Domingo.
Tainos	Indians, native of Quisqueya at the time of colonization.
Diablos Cojuelos	Colorful representation of Evil. People create different costume designs to disguise.
Merengue	Typical Dominican music, a very contagious rhythm.

SUCRE

Bitter Sucre

By Alex Bramwell

The city of the House of Freedom
has four names and forty languages
but all words are the same.
Rock strata show the birth and death
of liberty and conquest,
yet sweet is the sound
of broken bells that toll
for revolution.
Amidst the bones of history
students find their future
carved above their heads:
Hodie Mihi Cras Tibi –
Today Me, Tomorrow You.

TEGUCIGALPA

Tegucigalpa

By Claudia Patricia Sánchez Cárcamo

Why today
You smell of death
Tegucigalpa?

Enter your red sidewalks,
I no longer find
Comayagüela

Camouflaged twin
Forced to go
At one, two, three in the boot.

WASHINGTON DC

Swamp

By Kim Roberts

The Lincoln sinks into the Potomac
with a sigh. Constitution Avenue,
weary of constraint, reverts to canal,
complete with stink and Spring floods.

Swamp reclaims the grounds
of the Washington Monument, and river
reclaims the rest, filling with masts
that glided in from the Chesapeake Bay.

All the mere human efforts
of the Army Corps of Engineers
have come to naught. The Kennedy Center's
massive bunker, like a Soviet tank, slides

under the gurgling mud and the bridges dissolve,
their long lines of cars a dim specter.
Across the wide dirt roads downtown
Walt Whitman strides in his boots,

kicking up clouds of dust that eddy in his wake
—until he, too, wavers and melts
amid white columned buildings,
the classical ruins of grand intent.

WASHINGTON DC

Monuments

By Myra Skalrew

Today the moon sees fit to come between a parched earth
and sun, hurrying the premature darkness. A rooster in the yard
cuts off its crowing, fooled into momentary sleep.
And soon the Perseid showers, broken bits
of the ancient universe, will pass through the skin of our
atmosphere. Time and space are alive over our city.

Final eclipse of the sun, last of this millennium, our city's
brightness broken off. We have known other dark hours:
Here, coffin that slowly passes, I give you my sprig
of lilac—Lincoln's death, winding procession toward sleep.
We have known slave coffles and holding pens in yards
not half a mile from our Capitol, wooden palings sunk in earth

to guarantee none would escape. In this freest city. Oh if earth
could talk. Earth does talk in the neatly framed yards
where death thinks to lay us down to rest. Asleep,
the marker stones. But not the voices, jagged bits
of memory, shards of poems. Sterling Brown. Our
human possessions and all they've left us This whole city

sings their songs. Say *their* names. In this city
they are our monuments: Frederick Douglass, our
Rayford Logan, Alain Locke, Franklin Frazier, Georgia
Douglas Johnson, Paul Laurence Dunbar, May Miller: Not sleep
but garlands left to us. Montague Cobb, William Hastie. Yards
of names. And here, the place where we unearth

an immigrant father of seven. He leans down—no earthly
reason for his choice--to pick up his nearest child. A yard-long

rack of brooms behind him, a bin of apples. Not the sleep
of cold, but autumn in Washington. 1913 or a bit
later. He stands awkwardly on 4 ½ Street, S. W. as our
street photographer, who's just come by with his city

chatter, ducks beneath a dark cloth. Monuments of the city
behind him, he leans over his black box camera in time to capture
that moment when the child will play her bit
part, pushing away from her father like a boat from shore. In the sleep
of winter, years later, she will become my mother. What yardstick
by which to measure importance? To measure earthly

agency? Each of us has monuments in the bone case of
memory. Earth-
bound, I take my sac of marble and carry it down lonely city
streets where our
generals on horseback and a tall bearded man keep watch over
all their citizens.

ASIA PACIFIC

ABU DHABI

Abu Zhabi

By Navid Haider

If only my father could once again see,
the tallest towers of Abu Dhabi
If only now my father could see,
the breathing scars of Abu Dhabi.

Our homes now lie on renamed shores,
their frontiers were invisible before.
Our hearts lie open to neighbours like *Al Reem*,
and the islands of Abu Dhabi.

We are kissed and courted by more than the Emir,
the government alone does not gaze.
We are kissed and comforted by bridging the seas,
the sky-surfing Princes of Abu Dhabi.

A gift to *umma* would no longer be the rarest promises of jewelry;
Were she my own age,
she would no longer ask for your gifts:
the Independence of Abu Dhabi.

The *gurdwara*, *mandir* and church pray
with different names beyond our mosques.
We are hosts as you taught us, so that all may pray and eat—
the festive pride of Abu Dhabi.

If only my father could once again see,
he would hand me Orwell and say 'Navid,
You only see
the corporate eye of Abu Dhabi.'

AMMAN

Amman At Sunset

By Karl Schembri

Amman at sunset is a stubborn
teenage girl wanting to go clubbing,
against her adoptive parents' wishes
but wearing their makeup,
feigning maturity with its kohl-coloured eye-
lashes, blue finger nails reaching out to the
sky from the golden sea-less sand,
supplicating hand raised to be seen
and heard
in the chaos of regional voices
the harmless and the hardcore
dancing together under bright yellow lights
in the dry valleys.

ANKARA

For Sure

By Müesser Yeniay

So that I can't see the light of the day
God draws the curtain

I take my heart out of a wolf's mouth

I thought this place was all in stones
it is but all in darkness

cold, winters, leaves piercing
the body of a girl
—Ankara is alone like a widow

my body melts by the snow of sorrow
I am inadequate, for sure

even to be one person.

ASHGABAT

Ashgabat
By A.K. Welsapar

You know it is hard to be alone
To live anxiously with bruises in one's soul
I do not wish anyone to be cast away
from one's motherland and home

I do not get to see you Ashgabat
here alien sunrises, alien sunsets
I miss you badly in this distant land
When I see skies filled with stars

I remember the mountain wind
blowing on the moonlit nights
You are the most precious home
for all the Turkmen

Without your stars—like sea pearls
I am a lonely orphan, my heart aches
Perhaps that's my destiny
We are separated by cruel fate

I am not guilty of anything
I live far, nurturing my love for you
I know my own people think
I am a stranger living in a foreign land

I am doomed to suffer
Such is my destiny
That we live apart, but
I pine for you Ashgabat.

—*Translated from Russian by* Abhay K.

ASTANA

Winter in Astana

By Temirkhan Medetbek

It is so bitter cold here
that your spittle becomes ice
and face swells
as a pumpkin

your exposed ears freeze as rusted tin
you can't turn your head to the right or to the left
because of the terrible snowstorm
that beats like a puncher

the blowing snowstorm
dances like the devil
the cold freezes the city
into a prison

and when you tread on snow
dried as sand because of cold
it sounds as screech of a hungry man
who bites the edge of a dried bread

the trees are shivering with cold
even I have gone mad from the snowstorm
I want to wrap up myself in fur
and lie down

but before doing this
I would like to put fur coats
on all naked monuments in the city
except the one.

—*Translated from Kazakh by* Dauren Berikqazhyuly

BAGHDAD

Baghdad in Detroit

By Dunya Mikhail

On the 4th of July
here in Detroit
I hear the echo of Baghdad explosions
They say these are fireworks

Song by song
I scatter my birds
away from the fogs of smoke
They say these are ordinary clouds in the sky

A butterfly from the Tigris shores
alights on my hand
No bombs today to scare her away
They say this is the Detroit River

I enter a shelter
with the others in the crowd
We will exit at the end of the raid
They say this is the tunnel to Canada.

BAGHDAD

Baghdad Lapidated

By Salah Al Hamdani

I
What palm tree will be reborn from scorched earth?
Baghdad, my writing's wound.

Ancient city
built on dust
remember:
we were born from your narrow streets
        when the star of the penniless
        was sung by the fishermen.
Betrayed city
unfasten our childhood from the terraces of *Al Rachid* *
and gather the guillotined palms
on the shores of your body.

II
Violated city
you have nothing but the names of your martyrs on your walls
memory as revenge.

Orphaned city
I declare your injuries infinite
the cemeteries
from one hill to the other
make of you an open body
gaping
planted in uncertainty.

Oh Baghdad
cursed city

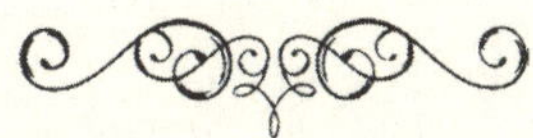

like you perhaps, I'll die among exiles
and I'll bind my tears to yours
and to those of your impotent gods.

*Haroun Al-Rachid, first caliph of Baghdad who encouraged culture and the arts. His reign, in the history of the Arab world, is known as the 'Golden Age'.

—*Translated from the Arabic by* Sonia Alland

BAKU

The Baku Wind

By Yeşim Ağaoğlu

how quiet, the furniture
and how the talkative wind howls
what is it he wants to tell us?
we should ask the furniture,
the clothes, the walls, the windows
their voice is muted, gentle
listen to their whisperings
its easy to fathom their secrets
come now, you chatterbox wind, tell us,
tell how you have wiped away everything thus.

—*Translated by* Nihal Yeginobali

BANDAR SERI BEGAWAN

The City of the God

By Abhay K.

The blessed city wrapped in a green blanket
on the banks of Sungai Brunei
welcomes first rays of the Sun
on its marble minarets and golden domes

across the lagoon children jump into the river
to swim to their schools, to welcome tourists
to Kampong Ayer—the Venice of the East
in Antonio Pigafetta's legendary chronicles

shines radiant the palace of light and faith
as faces of the shoppers at the Gandong Central
long noses of the proboscis monkeys
brighten up Brunei mornings in Pulau Ranggu.

Sungai	A river
Kampong Ayer	The village constructed on stilts over the Brunei river
Antonio Pigafetta	A traveller who accompanied the explorer Magellan
Gandong Central	The largest shopping complex in Bandar Seri Begawan
Pulau Ranggu	An island, which is home to long nosed proboscis monkeys

BANGKOK

Bangkok
By Abhay K.

Dystopia

I

A maze of stone, cement and steel
of highways and high rise condominiums

equipped with miniature pagodas
housing guardian ghosts and spirits

streets littered with massage parlours,
shopping malls

angels ever ready
to amuse flesh hungry guest-gods

II

As I wake up the sky has no birds
perched on the sky rises, steel cranes stare

where have the machines reached
while we sleep unaware

III

Mannequins stand in the metro
with wooden expressions

their distant gaze lost in space
their eyes occasionally blink

lost in gazettes
sound of speeding metro

is broken occasionally
by a recorded announcement—

'*please mind the gap between the train and the platform*
pee pee pee pee, the next station is Sukhumbit.

Utopia

A distant Ayodhya
where king Ram reigns

The Indralok on the banks of Chao Phraya
full of midnight Apsaras

where Indra rides his Airavat
to take a glimpse of the Siam Niramit.

Indralok	A heavenly abode of god Indra
Apsaras	Seductive cosmic dancers
Airavat	The mythical cosmic white elephant
Siam Niramit	A spectacular cultural show in Bangkok

BEIJING

The Negative

By Arthur Sze

A man hauling coal in the street is stilled forever.
Inside a temple, instead of light

a slow shutter lets the darkness in.
I see a rat turn a corner running from a man with a chair trying to smash it,

see people sleeping at midnight in a Wuhan street on bamboo beds, a dead pig floating, bloated, on water.

I see a photograph of a son smiling who two years ago fell off a cliff and his photograph is in each room of the apartment.

I meet a woman who had smallpox as a child, was abandoned by her mother but who lived, now has two daughters, a son, a son-in-law;

they live in three rooms and watch a color television.
I see a man in blue work clothes whose father was a peasant

who joined the Communist party early but by the time of the Cultural Revolution had risen in rank and become a target of the Red Guards.

I see a woman who tried to kill herself with an acupuncture needle but instead hit a vital point and cured her chronic asthma.

A Chinese poet argues that the fundamental difference between East and West is that in the East an individual does not believe himself

in control of his fate but yields to it.
As a negative reverses light and dark

these words are prose accounts of personal tragedy becoming metaphor, an emulsion of silver salts sensitive to light,

laughter in the underground bomb shelter converted into a movie theater, lovers in the Summer Palace park.

BEIJING

In Wintry Beijing

By Inara Cedrins

After Mongolian hotpot, we assemble our wraps
and reenter the dark hutong, where fine snow
falls like glitter, and above the walls
of soft gray stone sleek with ice
branches crackle, distant as an international connection.
We have not far to go, with linked arms
skirting the patches of ice: but I think of the boy named Light

lacing through the city on his bicycle
discerning fine-tuned as a bat the deep
secret places, as though on his forehead
a third eye pierced the darkness like a lamp,
the narrow hutongs unreeling like black and white
film, thin and transparent, each courtyard gate
framing a separate saga.

BEIRUT

As Two Stand

By Omar Sabbagh

For Faten

Tongue-tied cicadae
And the sky bereft its breath,
As evening settles,
        I settle the bets I owe

And walk with her –
        our two: in-tow:
        and no

Wrinkle
And no marring smear,
And no brim of boil or upset, and no
Hankering and no debt –
        and I wonder about

The snow that fell, small but happy bits
Of whitened smiles,
December passed, and yet
        how tulips shone

Upon their thrones
Of air and soil, where and when
We kissed that stone
Of the land we hark from:
Tongue-tied
        as Lebanon;

And was it true and was it

A forge and kiln
Of some brewed breast
Of sure imagination, one
Becoming two,

Or was it, or is it
Falling into many?

Are we the sores of that slipshod country?
Are we the roughshod feet
Of that bad tote
Of madly-splitting-sundry?

I don't think so.

I feel the clock ticks like no sentry
Known to mortal man
Or sad.

The time enters the wicket where
Batsmen swing. Now

Our teeming score
Will be all
And worthy
Of the pen's long-wrought drawl,

Or just scraps of notes,
        perhaps,
Splintered across the page,
Spelling nothing, nothing –

And how once we were
        so sure and sage,

Or close
And close to being so.

BISHKEK

Bishkek Angels

By Anatoly Kudryavitsky

Our past is our namesake;
our future, someone nameless.
In winter, Bishkek chimneys exhale
words of hope from the bygone times
when only one out of eight eyes had its
fair share of moonbeams.
And this not counting lunar eclipses
and vision disturbances.
Paper angels with silvery wings
dangle from the ceilings. They add
some lighting, and so does the phoenix
that once in a while bursts into flames
for the delectation
of yet another lost generation.

CANBERRA

Insiders/Canberra

By Michelle Cahill

A swathe of poppies, memorial to Darafshan,
 a father's odium for the rogue soldier.
In dust-winged chaos, machine-guns strafed at
 zero-hour, NATO games unplugged.
Those privates targeted by the Q&A talkback
 (Was the insider Taliban or insurgent?)
Does the sapper trust his foe? The never artless
 pernicious dare, a catch phrase retweeted,
the taskforce debriefed at Camp Coalition.

Official permits are redacted. I picture their final
 gaze drifting into outback ley lines
from black mesas, stony winter lakes, desert frost.

Wind wraps each homicide in Koranic ash. Why not
 embargo Sharia law from the civilising canon?
Homesick for a country of neo-fascists & anti-Muslim
 provocations, in a country of empty schools,
water shortages and zero literacy, we do unto Others
 because two hundred years of amnesia is
our excuse for genocide, because apostasy is our rule.

This poem is in memory of Australian soldiers killed in Darafshan, Afghanistan by insider attacks. They are commemorated in a Roll of Honour adorned with poppies at the Australian War Memorial in Canberra.

CANBERRA

Canberra
By P.S. Cottier

Built as a compromise, you dwell
between small hills that seem
an average of the notions of 'mountain'
and 'valley'. Inland, in a nation
that surfs towards the coast,
and cold, in a land tending to roast.
You are not Melbourne or Sydney.
Neither are you Tokyo or Paris.
Your high-rises trouble no birds,
kept to a moderate height, for
extremes are best avoided.
(Ignore the flap of that enormous flag,
subtle as a pterodactyl's wing.)
And birds do nest within your streets;
raucous cockatoos, who know little
of decorum, and parrots, courtesans
of the sky. Are you a city, Canberra,
or a garden? I hear you give
my question quiet consideration.
Your answer: A definite perhaps.

COLOMBO

A Trunk Call, Colombo

By Indran Amirthanayagam

We learned to say trunk calls,
long distance minutes with
the lost boy or uncle in England,

mufflered, sharing a bed
and hot water bottle with a girl
from Southampton, or Leeds

or London, the mystical man,
solitary occupant of a flat
venturing out into local pub

and company. When I think
of Colombo I remember
the family who left: Tambi,

poet and publisher
with his piss pot of gold,
naming Fitzrovia, that artist

retreat in Chelsea, London,
vital landmark in my Colombo,
English wagged and lobbed,

highland Scotch imbibed,
poetry learned from
the tradition in English –

my dad who wrote
the *Marriage of Continents*
told me when we left

the island that if
the English bigot calls
me a wog, not to worry,

he means I am
a Western Oriental
Gentleman. Not the case

back home where
the Tamil kept quiet,
on his guard, aware

of the minority's
precarious fortune,
perceived to have money,

or luck, or discipline,
or success in school
and business. That latent

disquiet is also Colombo,
named after the explorer,
whose mistaken discovery

of India occurred
in the island where I write
about that lost city, as far away

as a trunk call, a telegram,
McCarthy Nursing Home,
1960, a baby, composing

now from memory, Colombo,
a dream, a metaphor, a city
by the sea, white-porched,

white-walled, white coats
and tails, tropical evening dress,
the Grand Orient Hotel, father

in a cream suit, mother in long
white silk, a wedding, a child,
before expulsion from paradise.

DAMASCUS

Facing East

By Ruth Padel

This steel shell memorial to two lives,
a composer and his singer, looms at me
before sun-up like a guardian of the earth –
or a freezing North Sea re-run of the birth
of Aphrodite. *Dark*, says the sculptor
in her book. *Dark like a wave born*
backwards, shattering as it breaks.
Light and dark like life and death,
part shining and part rust, with movement
between colours as between the forms.
I creep in and run my hand along a frilled
bronze rim. A bivalve – two shells or
a single broken one self-joining at the core.
I think of the philandering sigh of ocean,
life-long partners betraying and forgiving
and Plato's cave: the fire, the sun

and how, arguing against his gift, he banned
artists for reflecting our world back
with a false beauty, making real unreal,
enticing us to take the shadow for the thing.
I gaze out, invisible as Echo,
at a lead gauze sea. Over my head
the breaker's cusp is a fanned-card silhouette.
Round the edge, letters punched out of metal
like finger-holes in a flute, write in paling sky,
I hear the voices of the drowned. Iron cloud
on the horizon splices day from night
like west from east. On the news
is flat-to-flat urban warfare in Aleppo

and air attacks on Gaza. Over here, in kitchens,
at the Tuesday evening pub quiz, on the bus or tube,
how quickly arguments flare up

even in England; even if we've never been
to what we call the middle of the east.
We identify. Some chasm through the centre
must be in and of us all: creatures of relation
and division, always wrong-footed by the past
on its bed of ice, the sub-tectonic clash
of ancient histories on common ground.
Suddenly I see this rifted arabesque,
a monument to music joined only at its core,
is all of us. *Harmonia*'s gift is cursed.
She can't help it, she's Aphrodite's child –
one false note and what you get is discord –
and her father, lord of war,
is Apollo's enemy. East or west, the first thing
looting soldiers smash (before starting on God's
perfect instrument, the larynx) is an oud or violin.

Sing the sadness and pain of *Sabah*,
the microtonal range of the *maqam.*
Hijaz, conjuring distant desert
and our longing for it. Sing the body:
tongue and teeth to whistle through,
palms to clap, lips to hum, vibrate
or tremble, and the fragile, mucus-laden
vox humana. Sing also of David's harp
placed sideways on the mountain, pitched
to catch wind blowing from rocks
below the tower of Lebanon which looks
toward the oldest city in the world –
whose sky burns indigo, dark-pearled
as strong espresso, above the fountain
in Umayyad Mosque. Where children
used to lick orchid-root ice cream

from *Bakdash Parlour* and now play
Asking-for-Papers-of-Identity-
at-Gun-Point. Where Saladin
and the head of John the Baptist
both lie buried. Where old men
with pewter urns poured tamarisk-
flavour liquorice in sudden jumps,
the way a flat stone skims water.
Al Fayha, Fragrant City, home
to *rosa damascena* and the damask plum:
these dawn-lit pebbles of the west
glow like your hieroglyph intarsia
whose weavers set compound floats
of warp and weft at angles to reflect
light scatter-wise, depending who you are
and where you're looking from.

What will survive are meanings we have found
in what the world has made. Like the calm
rufous freckling of those burnished steps –
infused with cardamom, I remember –
to Al-Hamidiyah Souq beside the citadel.
And at the top, strings of hanging flip-flops,
rosewood sets of backgammon like puzzle books
inlaid with mother-of-pearl, glinting gargoyle fish
and stalls of uncut samite, whose glitter-twill
depends on optic interference like the play of light
in Damascus Twist, the iron-plait steel
of sword blades and gun-barrels:
the mystery metal welded in carbon fire
which can cut a rifle muzzle or a hair
floating across a dagger. Whose laminate spirals,
acid-bitten into waves, resemble damask.

What would we be without desire for form?
Pattern keeps us safe. We look for omens in a flock
of redwing, the gods' will in dappled entrails,

the outline of a story in the stars. We break the line
to shape it, string catgut over membrane,
set up a ten-foot memorial
to music – a scallop shell, a pilgrim's prayer –
in shale of an eroding coast
and turn it east to face the storm.
Voices of the drowned. I watch dawn
gild the sea to iridescence. Sea-birds arc
and squawk and flicker-print the air.
Breakers roar on draining shingle.
Palmetto patterns dint the waves
from grey to silver, hyacinth and jade.
Making is our defence against the dark.

DHAKA

Tree Without Roots

(After 'You Hated Spain', by Ted Hughes)

By Ahsan Akbar

Dhaka frightened you. Dhaka
Where I feel at home. The raw daylight,
The sun-beaten faces, the sharp,
Edginess to everything, frightened you.

Your schooling had somehow neglected Bangladesh.
The martyrs of 1952, of 1971, and the floods
You could not appreciate the language,
Your soul was empty
Of the rustic Bauls, the rickshaw bells, and the hartals
Made your heart shrivel. Nazrul could not invoke
A blood rush, awake the rebel in you. Zainul
Held out a famine-struck, lean hand and you took it
Bluntly, indifferent to human feeling.

You did not criticise but you pitied
The endless beggars tapping your window,
You sniffed the history books like a condescending foreigner
Hoping to recognise your roots but somehow recoiled
As your love for the West asphyxiated you,
And your panic clawed back towards your Exeter days.

You came visiting every summer and the odd winter
Assumed yourself a tourist, armed with mineral water,
Mosquito repellent, beach shorts and funky flip-flops,
Watching with bewildered eyes and behaving awkwardly
At the butchered traditions, that somehow still held.
With the occasional stab to impress your pink tongue
Fortified by digestive tablets, you tried your luck

With the street savouries: *haleem, futchka, chotpoti.*
And I saw you vomit with food poisoning.

Dhaka, the city of mosques and shrines,
Had offéred you more than the customary rituals
But you did not hesitate to puncture the mystic,
Seeing only religious bigotry and fanaticism
And the sound of *azaan*
Was what annoyed you more than five times a day.

You told me this was the land of your dreams:
But the *kalboishakhi* was one
You dared not wake with, the incandescent spirit
No literature, no creative writing course had glamourised.
Perhaps this land is your nightmare, or perhaps,
Your wet dream, you did not realise
Monsoon had long spoilt your crisp bed.
Dhaka was what you tried to wake up from
And could not. You have been sleeping
Ever since; you knew you could afford
The luxury of distancing yourself from you.
You preferred to break out of your lineage
And have your real self yet to be found.

Yours is a hapless soul, not understanding,
Thinking it is still your prerogative
To remain in the happy world,
With your whole life waiting,
As a tree without roots.

DILI

Dili

By Abhay K.

Returning home
empty handed without fish
they say in Tetun
—the sea is big

the Cristo Rei stands
atop a distorted globe
above the cape (Fatucamas)
looking away in distance

at a heap of abandoned vehicles
after a thirteen years long peace mission
the children kick soccer ball
at the esplanade dotted with new embassies

women weave intricate tais
in bright, blazing colours
fishermen walk with their spears
effortlessly into the ocean.

Tetun A local language spoken in East Timor
Tais A traditional bright patterned cloth woven with intricate design by the locals

DOHA

Those Nights

By Dhabiya Khamis

All those nights
A nexus among cities of Loss

All those pale rhythms
Roving all ranges of Wilderness
Striking at a heart that speculates
The supremacy of fondness amidst sorrows
Amidst little revelation
Amidst the flutes of solitude
wreathed by the Jesus' garland

Wayfaring chose me; I chose it.
No horse, no Sahara, no sword
(In its sheath, though) traced the prey
as the Injurious Eagle did
as birds of carrions did

I became the vision that tricked me

Come tell the alienated one
amidst the heart of one's homeland
You die between two futures; between two dates,
No soil morsel; only dust to be taken

I kept all my secrets into the coffers
I laid my body into the coffin
My lips sealed tight in silence
As such, the Grand Secret buried with me
Little left for them, even that fluffed away
Amidst epochs, amidst their words

My death? Nay! Their death it be!
Had they a day before throwing me into the grave
they would have dug only their graves.

—Translated from Arabic by Abdul-Settar Abdul-Latif

HANOI

Hanoi

By Nguyen Bao Chan

The old tiles are startled
by the bustle of people
and the panic of the traffic.

Trees seem absent from the earth
sunshine parches the thresholds
the fragrance of Autumn is held in the lotus leaf
the cold wind carries my youth
through one more season
like a flash of lightning.

Winter has come to the crowded streets
covered with people in warm clothes
the leaves have left the almond-tree
its scrawny branches stoop in the chilly wind.

The lake ripples
brimful of stars
how sad the stars look
the dream is about to dissolve
as the wind blows across it.

The debris wakes
scratching the Royal Citadel
tears of an ancient time have turned to moss
growing a darker green.

ISLAMABAD

Islamabad

By Mehvash Amin

There are the gentrified mountains, not
Enough to unsettle, no, but enough
To be a logical foil for the gleaming city

Construed for a new nation.
Climb them, and you see it spread-eagle
Its green grid all the way to the lake

Beyond the brume and smoke of progress.
(They are clawing out dark earth to
Make way for a new air-rail, after all).

I think of decades ago, when I used to
Trek up here, and cycle on the smooth tarmac
Of new roads; I also remember

Heartache, and the loss that
Destroyed the neatness of
Geometry and grids, pummeled

Order into an ordinary chaos.
Beyond that, memories of my parents
taking me home as the streetlights

Dipped and rose luminously, the visible path
Of a heavenly comet – a child's imagination
Enmeshed with sleep. Then our new house,

On the same road as the Field Marshall's.
And seeing his handsome face rise balloon-like
From over the high wall of his estate –

He had built his garden above ground level,
You see, so he trod a higher earth than us.
Well, naturally, he had been President.

Then tales of fire and brimstone
Singeing the sky, when the army ammunition
Dump spit out death, cancelling out lives there,

But here, simply torpedoing a steel dolphin
Into our garden. It chose not to explode
With the desultory casualness of fate.

Twin towers fell elsewhere, and journalists
Rooting in the lobby of a hotel
Rushed to the rooftop when it was time

To pitch practiced stories.
Later, that same hotel would explode,
Shock waves curating plastics

Into furious artworks of destruction
And extending their clever skills to our house,
To morph glass into jagged waterfalls

And doorknobs into missiles. Too soon,
Our city became another city, loops of wire
Crisping its horizon, painted barricades

Brutalising its roads, insistently. Afghans
Who had hawked lapis and silver and
Wondrous kilims by the stream were

Herded off to their camps; grenades
Were tossed into smart restaurants
And diplomats went deep into fortified

Enclaves. That innocence of a new city,
That should have fetched hope, fought off
Doom instead, its encircled cancers

Spreading sly shoots beyond.
What happened in this city did not
Stay in the city, we all knew. Still.

Every time I ascend from my new
Home in the plains to my hometown,
Every time the blue mountains

In which the aircraft had slammed
Rise like some stone memory
My heart rekindles joss-sticks of old loves

And I wait to be returned to
That house on the hill, amidst poplars –
City of hope. City of embers My city.

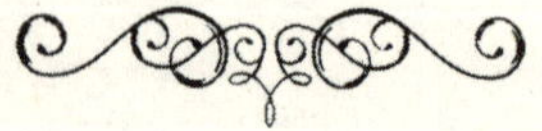

ISLAMABAD

City

By Ilona Yusuf

I

What might his thoughts have been - the dictator – benign, indulgent, envisioning the new city in the young nation as his eyes appraised roving field and thicket, lake and stream below the Margallas' shouldering rim, its slate slices folded snap-tight, its outcrops of yellow and grey and white amongst dense green casting a soft luminescence to the light, quickening flickerings from a childhood spent on the other side of these hills.

What might his thoughts have been, moulding the city for modern times, named for faith, thrusting into the certain future, its shining white blocks set in swathes of green, its single highway divided by arcs of lights, leading into nowhere and the hills.

The hills where history lay awaiting the restless hand of man to find its unexplored, unrecognized face: palm-fringed rock pools of meditating Sufis, still as silence; Buddhist caves; an ancient village hidden by a boulevard of the fledgling capital, with temple, gurudwara, mosque and shrine.

II

In the fledgling capital, government's apparatus: blocks laid out for officials, legions of functionaries and underlings; envoys and plenipotentiaries. Sophisticated village, strictly ordered, its avenues lined with saplings –rosewood and fiddlewood, kachnaar and bottlebrush, jacaranda and gulmohar, laburnum and maple, chinese tallow and silky oak.

III

Now, like the rock on which it rests the city begins to flex its muscles, jostle the shapes it was laid into, the mould in which

it was set. Like limestone, water melts its hardness, opening passageways where once there were dead ends. Like limestone, cliques split and crumble; fold and splice.

Like the streams that run through its streets, settlers cross and crack the strata, growing arteries north and south. Quietly, new clans send down roots, where surety and power did not think to question. Like the tremors that rock the city, send stone and pebble sliding, turmoils ripple its foundations, outsiders slowly, then swiftly, gathering where no one thought to look.

Note: like Brasilia and Chandigarh, Islamabad was conceived and built as a new capital city, using a grid formation, in the early nineteen sixties.

Dictator Field Marshal Ayub Khan, Pakistan's first military ruler, who made the decision to build a new capital city north of Karachi, Islamabad

Margallas A range of hills which flank the city. Since the area was under the sea, there are many fossils and limestone formations

JAKARTA

Jakarta

By Indah Widiastuti

Jakarta is an urban womb
of every hope born

every one survives here
in the underworld of shadows

while the city struggles
to keep its legends

against the silent scream
the red mumbling hum

of hawkers, street musicians, beggars
this metal-scape is a memorial park.

Jakarta was once *Jayakarta*
and its streets were filled

with greens and drupes—*Menteng*
Gambir, Marunda, Rambutan Lenteng

it was a vintage sketch
of the rural landscape

with coconuts bays
where children played carefree.

It wakes up now every morning
with a stern and grumpy face

staring at concrete high rises
disguised, wearing masks

people are reborn here everyday
to survive the heartless regimes

pale in the glare of LCD billboards
a solitary moon wishes to be adored.

Gambir, Menteng, Lenteng, Marunda, Rambutan
varieties of tropical indigenous fruit
Jayakarta Sanskritised name of Jakarta

JERUSALEM

Terror In Jerusalem

By Asa Boxer

Terror lives in the cornerstones, and in the small
monuments around what seems like every bend.
Terror at the children murdered in their dawdling.

A small, cold slab of stone marks the morbid place
where young muscles squirmed a pace
like worms against the dust; and then,
like worms, fell flaccid and gave up.

A candle flickers by the stone; its heat throbs
like the heart that beat the blood to earth.
And the flame that tugs and flashes
on the wick, flashes and tugs on the collective brain.

These children are the grim cement of a nation,
the crumbling stonework, the shaky foundation.
Their bones are the hardware underlying the infrastructure;
they are the fodder, fuelling the slogans and campaigns.

The valley of Gehenna is fertile;
centuries of infant sacrifices, and it burns green.
Now, the surrounding desert is thirsty.
And not an Abraham hesitates over his Isaac;

not a soul feels the angel's restraining hand.
Instead, the radio keeps a finger on the pulse,
and we listen for its death tolls and commands.

JERUSALEM

In Jerusalem

By Mahmoud Darwish

In Jerusalem, and I mean within the ancient walls,
I walk from one epoch to another without a memory
to guide me. The prophets over there are sharing
the history of the holy...ascending to heaven
and returning less discouraged and melancholy, because love
and peace are holy and are coming to town.
I was walking down a slope and thinking to myself: How
do the narrators disagree over what light said about a stone?
Is it from a dimly lit stone that wars flare up?
I walk in my sleep. I stare in my sleep. I see
no one behind me. I see no one ahead of me.
All this light is for me. I walk. I become lighter. I fly
then I become another. Transfigured. Words
sprout like grass from Isaiah's messenger
mouth: 'If you don't believe you won't be safe.'
I walk as if I were another. And my wound a white
biblical rose. And my hands like two doves
on the cross hovering and carrying the earth.
I don't walk, I fly, I become another,
transfigured. No place and no time. So who am I?
I am no I in ascension's presence. But I
think to myself: Alone, the prophet Muhammad
spoke classical Arabic. 'And then what?'
Then what? A woman soldier shouted:
Is that you again? Didn't I kill you?
I said: You killed me...and I forgot, like you, to die.

—*Translated from the Arabic by* Fady Joudah

KABUL

The Kabul

By Reza Mohhamadi

I was a word abandoned in an old battered book,
a word forgotten by politics, by love and the world.

The poets fled from me. All of my letters detested me,
deserting me for other words without looking back even once.

Just like that I was alone, a ghost-word that lacked its letters,
lonely, the terrible sound of frenzied centuries

for company, only the sound of the slaves, of the dead,
of the arrows of time flying, flying and flying.

You (o my true love) came with your fierce mouth
and hands of ten desolate fingers and found me

and the whole world did shout for me.

KATHMANDU

Kathmandu And Her Affairs

By Cathal Ó Searcaigh

Day breaks out and she wakes me up suddenly
With a cock-crow kiss!
Looking out from the top window
I spy her in the streets, parading her morning saffron sari.
Her breath in traffic flow, pure draught of heat.
She's on her feet now, no time to rest,
Her clutch about her;
She rouses them with a noisy jackdaw voice, puts the skids under them,
Humouring them so that they might face this day breezily –
A day rising out from the yellowing globe of her eye.
Lunch hour, from the hotel balcony, I see her
Stretched in slumber,
Her urban contours lying awkwardly, dog tired,
Her bazaar bosom heaving, exhausted,
The dangerous laneways of her combed tresses.
Today the poor are huddled
In the backstreets of her cloak, fretful,
Their wants, their needs pierce her
And how she sighs over and over again when the strong
Walk all over the weak – kid goat teaching its mother to bleat.
Tutelary spirit of street shrines, wonder-woman of broken palaces,
Wise one of crumbling courtyards.
A while ago her sky-eyes darkened and she wept with consternation
Seeing her family rising up in rebellion
Against all oppressors.
The softness of prayer in her wild words
As her body supports scaffolding –

Stink of pus in her bones –
In spite of this she sings a song of hope
In the cries of protesters, blossoming tongue of youth.
Evening. Pagoda-shaped she is,
Bright gems glisten in her ears;
She walks a stately walk among her own, blesses them
With incense chatter: hear the little peals of laughter
As she banters with market ladies, fiery eyed.
Night. She spreads the bright
Head-dress of darkness
Over all, her satin cloak
Encrusted with silver brooches, an amber moon
Her torch, traffic horns her hum.
To her I will lift my eyes, my soul's nurse,
When midnight rings
And I stretch my limbs; she comes to me with a sleeping-draught
Full of giddy sparks from the sky. As she departs
She leaves a star in the window, sweet and soft as her kiss.

—*Translated from the Irish by* Gabriel Rosenstock

KATHMANDU

The Eight-Eyed Lord Of Kathmandu

By Abhay K.

After J. Milton Hayes

I

There is an eight-eyed, benevolent, compassionate lord
atop a hill to the west of Kathmandu.

There is a garden of dreams in the town
a beautiful girl waits there

for the return of her love
perhaps long dead

and the self-born compassionate lord
forever gazes down.

II

A cacophony of dust and smoke
my arteries clogged with wheels
defaced, decomposed faces stare
blankly at me, poison runs in my veins
I doubt if I am the same earthly paradise
born out of the sword of Manjushree
or *Bhanubhakta's Kantipuri, Amravati Nagari.*

III

In the still of night
a solitary dog barks

a clear face flickers
a clock ticks
the deepest desires and gravest fears
come out of hidings
tremors awaken my conscience
the moon enters into my being
a clear face flickers

a solitary dog barks
in the still of night
a sonorous voice
pierces the darkness of my being.

IV

When it rains here
it rains bliss
I wish it rained for a hundred years
and each drop seeped in
cleansing me of concupiscence
letting a thousand Buddhas bloom
within.

KUALA LUMPUR

Ghazal – Leaving Your City

By Sharanya Manivannan

I augur these nights for stars that cannot be seen in the sky
of your city I wake counting the dawns that trickle to the day –
I'm leaving your city.

My hunted heart consumed by an undertow of longing for a
landscape not a cremation ground for all the dreams I lay to
waste, believing your city.

Sod your government and its godless lies, there is history
here in the smoke the coke the mirrors, the golden waltzes still
conceiving your city.

Don't call me citizen. Don't call this home. Exile is the only
song I've ever known. Let me go now, I'm tired of believing,
deceiving your city.

Remember me in demarcations, remember me radiant, searing.
Glimmering in borders, partitions, trespasses, my sweet broken
heart cleaving your city.

My earthen body electric, receptacle, bewildering in its need –
I walk these streets now, open, receiving your city.

For tonight I'm here, dreaming of and drinking in the heat,
the beat and all the pretty skyscraper lights and darknesses
weaving your city.

But how I've been betrayed and I don't intend to forget the
bitterness, the spilled blood and the black chimes of bigotry
sieving your city.

My time here has come and gone. I take with me now these
torrents of memory.
While you search for stars you cannot see, I'll be
retrieving your city.

Sharanya says, this is all you need know: on the day I leave I
will wake here, and close my eyes to sleep in another nation,
grieving your city.

KUWAIT CITY

The Journey

By Shurooq Amin

Frail tremors snare
a porcelain sea
in green-glaze

intricate sails
bleached bright
over a verdure

tinge sifted with
powdered orange-gold
dust plucked

from a curtain-folded
sky scuttling across
the green-glazed
porcelain sea

viscid in this
humidity

a new slant of sun
and spits of
darting water

scrape the
imagination

nudge mangosteen-hard
perpetuity

swift falcon cries
imbue undefiled
paned beauty

all in a vitreous broth
encrusted with
sail-cinders and
a wondrous olivine
nebula in this
water-soluble state
of Kuwait.

MALE

Male

By Ibrahim Waheed 'Ogaru'

I

Male Forty Years Ago

A chicken scratched for insects
On clean white coral sand
Swept by women with smiles
with coconut-leaf brooms.

A house was a coral building
Thatched with coconut leaves
Where families had for lunch
fresh-barbecued fish

Everybody knew everybody else
Cared for all and smiled meeting each other
Doors were left open
and food was shared with happiness.

II

Male Today

A little island where I was born
A chicken lies huddled
In a freezer in a clean plastic bag
Where scooters race past in a mad race

A house is a small apartment,
Air-conditioned to perfection,
Where families have for lunch
Hot dogs spiked with mayo

We are all strangers to each other
Scared, we frown at each other
Doors have to be double-locked, tight
and food, when offered, is dumped with suspicion.

MANAMA

The Bahraini Child

By Ali Al Jallawi

Like a dove
Which lands on your palms
And drinks from the bowl of your breast and mouth
Thus my heart.

Over its fingers, your breast closes a warm flower
And it returns as a child
Saying to his toy:
God will punish you.

Back to front he wears his clothes
And falls asleep on himself.

Like two sparrows
Squabbling over a wheat kernel fallen from his hand.

Like two larks
Which peek out from her shirt…
He feared his lanterns would be seen
By those standing
He said, 'I don't have' – pointing to his pocket – 'my language here.'

He started running, the path slipped from under him
From his hand, the sea poured
His knees dropped onto a star
And nearby, a rose cried.

She arose and lifted his face
And her laugh broke off inside him

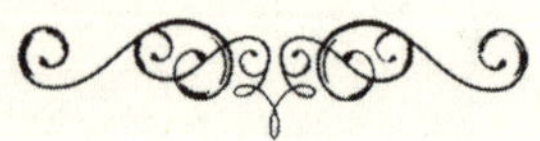

He pulled out the thorn
And shyly he licked God's nectar

One child she will find
Stealing the almonds from her hair
And hiding them in his eloquence

Another left the field drawn on the wall
Without turning off the river
And the charcoal's remorse drowned him

He said to nobody
Their flowers were thirsty...
But nobody was setting the roads aflame with his steps

Like...
When he stumbled over the dream and the path
He started kicking their ribs
The house, the roads and his neighbour's trees followed his
steps

Like two sycamores
Like doves
Landing on a wire of his ideas
God poured from his chest
His knees dropped onto a star
And nearby, Manama cried.

MANILA

Manila to Me

By Marra PL. Lanot

Is the shattered glass of Intramuros
Where my head was once dipped in
A basin of holy water and salt.
It is the church thrice shaken by earth-
Quake, twice plundered by war;
Its walls held sacred by little
Brown hands that burn cold in the sun,
White under moon and swaying palms.
It is the rugged road kissed
By small brown feet of children
Shouting old jars and papers,
Chasing away bitches to canals,
Whistling a common tune they hear
From the other dingy room.
Beneath the sky flower barong-barongs,
Kangkong and nilad from a pool of
Mud, frogs, mosquitoes beside
The railway that howls at midnight
When a train passes to el norte del sur.

It is Manila rich with the warm
Spit of barbers and shoeshine boys,
Of guitars strumming for stolen chickens,
Of zarzuelas and firing goons,
Maria Elenas glowing with emerald,
Maria Elenas cussing with each
Tug at the hem. This is Manila
That knows the quiet grave
Beckoning stronger than neon lights
Or steel or smoking factories.

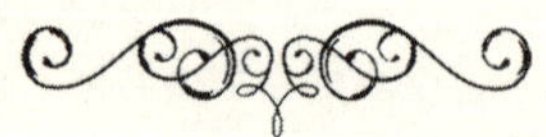

Manila that is mother earth
For it is brave enough to own
Heroes killed for unremembered cause,
Men who slit throats merely to survive,
Brother hating brother while eternally
Creating myths around Maria
Or dalaga in distance, drops of ugliness string
The loveliness that is Manila to me.

MUSCAT

Muscat

By Abhay K.

Cryptus Portus, Amithoscuta
the crown of the strait of Hormuz
strong scented rare musk

a delicious date
spread over mountains and mosques
its street filled with rolling tongues

Alladin's lamp, wish and
a waiter runs out like a genie
carrying *shawarma, sambosas*, falafel

women in *shylas*
each uniquely wrapped
some around face, others simply tucked in the tail

girls in white button-down
boys in *dishdasha* and *kummah*
at two opposite ends of the town

a child walks alone towards the city centre
to buy popsicles, chips and candies
while adults watch movies subtitled in Arabic.

NAYPYIDAW

Urban Renewal

By Ko Ko Thett

double it or nothing, you and your hybridism
your face needs to be lifted, the sprawl beyond
your subconscious needs to be gentrified, wasteyard
shall be renamed goldengarbageland, dig tunnels for
an extensive sub way network for your pigeon
commuters, the public transport in your brain should
be integrated, a fence for hate padlocks right in front
of the white wedding chapel, graffiti shall be encouraged
on the inner walls of your empty chest, dog parks for dogs
amusement parks for amusements, child-friendly facilities
for the parents of the children who may never grow up
bingo halls for all ages and sexual preferences, clear the
woods on the city's fringes for nine-hole golf courses
logging shall be licensed to make way for streamlined
taxiways for international arrivals, plant garden plants
in every department stores, to age is to get less serious
about life, to die is to be incinerated to be reincarnated
a multi-purpose stadium for metal concerts and the
vipassana for the masses, two ivory chopsticks shall
be contracted to conduct the people's symphony orchestra
a brand new opera house to be modelled after a durian
it shall be named after our own houseman, a nine-lane
boulevard of broken bones shall be the city's artery
hot-beds will be moved to the out-skirts, council houses
will be patched up with thatches, aquatic centres for those
who will learn to splash, splash and splash, waves of all sizes
shall be regenerated and recycled, the monument of doubt
in the plaza shall be torn down, in its place the leaning tower
of certainty will be erected, crocodiles shall be released in
the moat of the pentagonean presidential palace

all administrative quarters of your soul shall be made
sound-proof to prevent the intrusion of street noises
malling, walling, enthralling and everything else
that will make your cosmopolis
your oober-capital

NEW DELHI

Delhi

By Abhay K.

I

My smell, my nakedness
entices hordes of human flesh
from faraway lands —
traders, emperors, marauders.

I pose nude
up on the hill
below a feast of eagles —
possessed, intoxicated.

II

I am the city of cities.

A city of invaders, conquerors
merchants, immigrants—
they twinkle on my horizon
appear, disappear
as words written on a palimpsest.

I am the city of ruins.

Look carefully
at my mausoleums, cemeteries, tombs
count them all if you can
how many lie buried here
who ruled me once.

I am the city of *Satya*, *Shanti* and *Nyaya*.

My streets bear these names
but the Truth is—
criminals roam my streets in Peace
and my women perpetually seek Justice
in the city-courts.

Satya Truth
Shanti Peace
Nyaya Justice

PHONM PENH

A Letter to Phnom Penh

By Chath Piersath

You survived. And you are thriving. Everywhere now, you are full of life. Out of the darkness, you bounced back to light, to freedom, resilience and hope. Paved roads and skyscrapers are the future. The darker times are past now. The years of genocide and human cruelty are over. Or is it?

I remember it was 1972 when a Vietcong killed my father in a battle. His body was taken to one of the temples where all dead soldiers were cremated. My mother took me along by train to claim his ashes.

My aunt's villa had multiple floors, brick walls and plastered concrete. Our village home was built on stilts with thatched roof. We slept on a mat on bamboo floor. People in the city lived differently, unlike the rural poor.

There was plenty of food. Boiled corn. Rice porridge in a bowl, with coagulated chicken blood cubes and pig intestines and steamed bean sprout. Peace. Cars filled the city's streets. People strolled on big boulevards, in parks full of flowering trees and lived in big beautiful villas. Rich people in chic clothes rode cyclos.

My aunt's sons were Lon Nol soldiers like my father. I didn't understand then that they, too, could be killed. I wanted to be a soldier when I grew up. It was 1975. My mother and neighbors followed the news closely from Phnom Penh. On the radio, they said the war was coming to an end.

The Khmer Rouge won. People were shouting with glee, peace is here. Peace is here. No more war. They waved the white flag for

peace. This rejoicing, however, was short lived when a gun was fired. The radio went silent. Leave your home, said the Khmer Rouge. Take nothing. We will be gone for a few days 'til the American bombing stopped.

A few days turned months and years. We lost all counts of days and weeks. We knew only hard labour and starvation. There was not a day we didn't think of food. I thought of the rice porridge and the noodles in Phnom Penh. My mouth watered tasting my mother's tapioca, sweet tamales wrapped in banana leaves. Hard cooked rice freshly scooped from a pan and chicken curry and grilled fish dipped with shredded mango sauce. I prayed to be spared from hunger.

The next three years, eight months and twenty days, to be exact, there was no news, no radio or music. No movies, but Pol Pot's Angkar and Maoist songs marching us to our death.

The Vietnamese invasion saved us. The children were free to run, and running we did, as far as we could, Looking for surviving relatives. My little sister was alone covering her ears, hiding from bombs. Then we found our mother. She survived. We hugged tightly. A few siblings also survived.

In 1980, I fled to Thailand through the jungle and survived again. I went to the US in 1981 where I learned how to read and write English and lived the American Dream, thinking of home. Where? When I was old enough, home was where Western accounts described as Cambodia.

They were telling me about my own history and what I had lived through. They said American bombs fell from the sky. Tons and tons of them. Hiroshima and Nagasaki combined. People were murdered. There was a genocide, they said. 1.7 million people perished. I went to see the movie, The Killing Fields, saw myself in it and cried.

I returned for the first time in sixteen years in 1994. Together at last as beggars, prostitutes and land mine victims, sharing AIDS and corruption. There were two landmines to every Cambodian. Two times a country of twelve million people. A city of squalid and filths.

The heartbeats of life returned. Our people are happy and free. Democracy has its own chains but without genocide and the torture chambers. Maybe they still exist, but in different disguises. Life is still good as long as there's peace, and as long as it's not as black or as cruel as the Khmer Rouge. Anything is better than the Khmer Rouge.

PORT MORSEBY

Port Moresby In High Savannah

By Russell Soaba

Sun on light mist, the yellow
hills. Smoke, mucous sky.
An early riser casts
a glance at the sleeping sea
and yawns.

The day is a tired old earth
panting eighty degrees Fahrenheit.
The afternoon brings in dusty wiry
hair, and stomachs that are empty.
Then dusk;
burnt sienna clouds, sky:
a solitary mud lake.

We could love this city
a fluorescent lagoon
of suburban tropicalities;
areca drug days
bahasa sunsets
and no betel nuts
for the gods.

The fall of evening blinks out
silhouetted signs:
itambu
nogat wok.

itambu	do not trespass
nogat wok	there is no work

PORT VILA

Port Vila

By Abhilash Surendran

Like dragonflies in the light, they danced
under no duress, beyond words, beyond tomorrow,
the future holds the key, they can't see
they live because they are children of the Sun

Through open windows and creaking doors
they stared at me, like a naked leprechaun falling from the sky
their eyes—uncut diamonds, pierced my camera,
they asked—*'Man blong India, why yu come by?'*

PYONGYANG

A Silent Poem

By Alex Bramwell

I caught the train in East Berlin –
its last stop was Pyongyang.
Through windows scratched with slogans
I saw a city that was not a city
but a monument, a temple
with no God,
and a Leader long buried,
still standing.
On dirt-free streets filthy air was
filled with song from loyal voices.
There were no whisperers,
there were no lies –
only the official version.

RIYADH

The Desert Bride

By Ashjan Hendi

Set me up a place somewhere
under the pure sky
where night dreamily hugs shy stars.

Set me up a place
            in the silver moonlight
to sing along with the desert
night after night
and dance along with hopes
to make flowers bloom.

Set me up a place
in a homely and warm tent
just like the old days,
to listen to Shahrazad
telling tales of Arabian nights
about the beautiful Riyadh
            the desert bride.

Set me up a place
where songs evoke memories
and love blossoms
in the heart of Riyadh.

Let my dreams reach the sky
please don't wake me up
and don't ask me why
dreams should be sweet
when they come true
in luscious Riyadh.

Set me up a place
under a golden sunshine
I desire to kiss the coming day
yours and mine,
to celebrate it joyously
the way Bedouins celebrate rain
falling in the desert.

Just take me there
to the home of my heart
my very self and my senses,
the place where sand celebrates
the golden sunlight in love poems
and poetry tempts birds
to sing every morning and night
to Riyadh, the desert bride.

Come fly with me
let's fly there
on Sindbad's rug
to see the new city
to explore
the way the desert treasures
love, pureness, simplicity
insistence, dignity.

Let's fly with the zephyr
dreams are always over there
in the golden sunlight.

SANA'A

The Book of Sana'a

By Abdulaziz Al Muqaleh

The spirit of this city floats
On the water of years.
Do not wake her
Let her moan while her children drown.
Do not light her pale alleys,
For the streets are still wet
With the sweet blood of martyrs
Who died for their homeland,
And turned the pages of life too soon

Let her sleep to forget
Let her sleep to remember
do not scratch with words
The tomb she has erected
for her grief.
Above it moan corpses
Below it they are lost.

—*Translated from the Arabic by*
Huda Fakhreddine and Jayson Iwen

SEOUL

How to Eat in Seoul

By Kim Gyeongmee

Be a heart like the bean sprouts boiled to the core
Never spill a single grain of the quiet in the shade of rice
Eat it all in silence though there be no height of sugar in endurance
Suffering-don't tear away its crust as if were a loaf of sandwich bread
Let there be just one side dish, one called diligence

Am I doing something useless again all of a sudden
Will I make it to the end of my natural life
Though the pebbles of fear and regret crunch between your teeth
though the days are like the black inside of anchovies when
you feel like squandering it all and everything
take in more of that light in the eyes, gentle like vegetables

Slither out like a fish even at the regularity of life's despair and
straighten your mind and body like a pair of chopsticks
Swallow well yet another life
like a sip of water after a meal

SINGAPORE

To Go To S'pore

By Alvin Pang

After Zagajewski's 'To Go to Lvóv'

To go to S'pore. Which station
for S'pore, if not in a dream, at dusk, when rain
glistens on chrome. When Mass Rapid
Trains and Light Rail Trains are borne
to all corners. To leave in a hurry for S'pore,
night and day, in August or in May, but early,
but only if S'pore exists, if it is to be
found within the bounds
of this island and not just
in the colour of my passport, of my smart card;
if the smell of rain trees after thunderstorm,
of angsana, of frangipani, still lingers
like fresh smoke; if the canals brim
and grumble like epithets in Hokkien, vanish
beneath ground. To pack up and go, to leave
and never look back, at 5 p.m. to cease
like shop windows, while beneath the whirl
of fans in coffee shops, geckos chatter
their politics. But the office tower rises, straight
as the law, and everyone standing
in its shadow, and a mop and bucket leaning
on window glass, and our dream which hadn't
come yet, only concrete, and litter-bins and the
rainbow pulse of new pubs set to music, the low
bass tremble of bumboats, rocking.
Always too much of S'pore, no one
could fathom the depths of its neighbourhoods,
walk the inside trails between each block and hear

the creak and hiss of each brick speaking, scalded
by sun, at night the city's muteness, the dead
stillness in Shenton Way unlike that of temples
where monks keep silence full of unseen rivers.
In Liang Seah street history spilled
in unlit stairwells and on window louvres
swinging and shutting by themselves, in china
blue ceramic tiles, in flour, in the smell of eggs,
the form of feathers plastering the walls, in green
muck collecting in rusty pipes, fronds growing
where laundry once sprouted and the streets
played percussion and the air singed, the procession
of the devout sang like kings of the world
toward the temple gates. People in such frantic joy
they didn't want to stay indoors. So much life
it burst and flooded every street, it cracked the sky in
thunder and fireworks, the new year lived over
and over. My granny as she stood at the window
calling for my father, dinner ready and
steaming in the evening light and neighbours
shouting from windows, watching out for
trouble and the next meal and nothing tentative
as hope. An uncle slaved himself blind
reading by candlelight, while my father was out
catching fireflies. The health inspector came
and my grandfather bought him a drink
and covered the cockroaches with his sole, and
got away with it. Even then
there was too much of S'pore, it overflowed
each drain, came down as rain, so much and yet
none; what was there spawned, grew, cut
into shape not without love and now the green
June springs from every square, verdant wigs
pulled over everything. Weeds, attap, kampong
and five-foot way fell away as the towers rose,
pushing out above the temples, people shuffled on,
handbags and wallets full of tomorrow,

and every estate growing into each other,
and everyone a leaseholder, and now in a hurry
to just go, and somewhere to come and go from,
S'pore tugged every which way,
S'pore clutched in the small palm of the sea,
becoming and flowing in like tears, tides, currents,
rivers run beneath the surface everywhere.

SUVA

The Happy City
By Sudesh Mishra

Yes, it rings true: we are the happy few.
We have been kept in the dark for so long
We see in it the first stirrings of dawn.
Thus the light we know not to be true
Equals the night we know not to be false.
We're grateful to our leader for his gift,
For demonstrating in diverse decrees
The wisdom of rugging up when it's hot,
Of peeling skin when the mercury sinks.
Our officers and chefs embrace his lead.
They praise the wonders of expired milk
And hail maggots animating their steak.
Their happiness is as one with his mood
For they see in the dark the spark of dawn.

TASHKENT

Tashkent

By Hamid Ismailov

'Heh, Fuzuli, are your tears really not needed by you?'
—Fuzuli, 16th century

Aimless wandering.

Has summer come?
In your life you'll still write another
twenty five books in the little square
among the mass of stone, ugly memorials.
Some concrete piece, the existence of a memorial
left by the builders,
turns into the absurd
as though, yes, say as though, in as far as
even if the thought ends
the yearning to continue it
does not end.
Shall I go into the dining room
and soak my hardened
brains in tea
so as to pour into my thought?

Here no one needs you,
but this is just the
w
i
d
t
h
and the
l e n g t h
of the fact that you need no one.

TBILISI

Streets of Tbilisi

By Sabrina Masud

She said, 'I love to travel in the night in dark streets of Tbilisi',
and I asked – what do you mean by 'love', do you mean
to say you wouldn't mind letting your mind travel at the
touch of a pebble underneath your toe, sniffing for the
Black Sea resting her hip so far away from your finger
tips, and exhaling when the wind trots a step away simpering
for the echo off the Byzantine dome trapping its voice or
do you mean to say you wouldn't deny that 'love' that
makes you pick up that pebble and throw it to shatter
the light into pieces, or does the straight symmetry of
the lanes make you whimper for a curve here
there or do you mean to say you would allow the
autumn wind to brush past your thighs and tug
at your skirt or is this 'love' not as mundane
as being pushed against a brittle wall of a balcony
overhead, legs almost parted or would you frame
the shadows of one street leading on to the other
and the faint scent of T'one blazed morning bread
pulled out of your navel, or do you mean the 'love'
that coarse lips sucked out of your breath while
you were too engrossed in the scent of morning dew
and forgot the chokha clad rebel pressing hard against you,
because the trinity of samaia inked your inheritance to a
woman who once was a King...
...is this the 'love' you speak of?

T'one A Well-shaped traditional Georgian oven
Chokha A traditional Georgian attire
Samaia A Georgian folk dance performed by three woman

TEHRAN

Turning the Page

By Mimi Khalvati

'The mighty mountain-sentinel Demavand ... becomes so familiar and cherished a figure in the daily landscape, that on leaving Teheran and losing sight thereof the traveller is conscious of a very perceptible void.'

— George Nathaniel Curzon,
Persia and the Persian Question (1892)

This grey
is made more bearable
by the thought of sun
on your own brown skin
just over the horizon

and this loneliness,
looking over its shoulder
at its own old absence,
looks forward too
to a merry death

and the lucky West Indian
in a language that can be,
when all's said, at least read
by oppressors, hopes
to honour his grandmother;

but what if every time
the thought was struck dead
as the tree where you kissed
in the mule-shade
of a glade in Damavand?

What if the city
that gave credence to your sickness
were as vanished as the home
you took for granted you would bless
with success and happy children,

were now as alien as the dun
of another tongue, of freckled skin?
Would you turn to the dying –
take a leaf from their book?
To history, Russia for example?

How dead would a page be
without the smile you drew
(in brackets) on the face
of a sun, of a country
on the other side?

THIMPHU

Going to Thimphu

By Abhay K.

Wind batters my car windows
as I travel along the river Paro

intricately painted houses as carved marmalade
black wooden windows, painted walls

men in gho, women in kira
play with bow and arrow

two girls sit along the highway combing their hair
newly wed royal lovebirds smile from giant billboards

stray dogs and cows languor along the road
a ceremonial gate welcomes me to Thimphu

a sculpture of a monkey riding an elephant
four-five storeyed houses painted in mute colours

snooker billboards, car service centres
furniture shops populate the street

the city turns silent at dusk, shops shuts, traffic halts
only Tashichhu Dzong shines bright at night

a long valley descends down the river Raidak
as a masked cham dancer

in the courtyards of Tashichhu Dzong
the dragon king reigns Dru U wearing the raven crown.

TOKYO

Tokyo

By Jan Napier

In a certain country unstable as its geology
        nights are charred paper.
Whispers transform them to flakes of ash
        the wind lifts and whirls like fairy skirts.
Burglars and the merely clumsy
        walk through walls as easily as dreams.
People have skin the colour of sun through honey.
Men neat as parcels of fish prepared by wives
        with downcast eyes know that humility
and hands are the only weapons
needed when respect is its own blade.
Camellias infuse their days with ceremony
        yield longevity and good health.
Art is the scalene triangle sun   moon   earth
        or carved on the teeth of dead giants
in a flowery and expensive complexity
also seen in the general's treatise on war.
A fondness for animals pervades.
Poets compose short verses about frogs
        a child's pony appears at table
a stray cat is taken in and fattened.
Counterfeit money is gifted to ghosts.

These things come in waves.

ULAANBAATAR

The Sparrows of Ulaanbaatar

By G. Mend-Ooyo

The last leaves tear from the trees and fly away.
A flock of sparrows come in to take their place.
A multitude of eyes glisten like bright chalcedony,
looking from outside the window at the flowers in the room,
these dear sparrows are lucky with their canopy of cliffs,
thinking about the dark blue hollows of their country.
They do not brush against the white clouds of autumn.
They do not sing in the blue of the sky, out on the peaceful
steppe
Now, the sparrows are becoming city-dwellers,
will they make their nests in the towers which reach the stars?
While I sip my hot coffee from a china cup,
quietly I sigh seeing these birds.
My eyes see magic clips of new songs on the TV.
Nomadic journeys unroll century after century.
Nomads from the wild steppe head for Ulaanbaatar.
Thousands of hills are thinking amidst the grasses.
From everywhere they're moving to the city,
even the sparrows gladly follow them from the north.
The guard-dogs follow behind, sniffing the ground.
Just how will these creatures feel, now they're in the city?
The sparrows peck at breadcrumbs in the balcony.
They crane their necks to peer inside my room.
They gaze at the picture of the wild steppe on my wall.

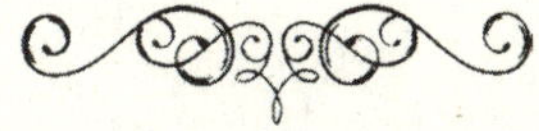

VIENTIANE

Vientiane in Twelve Haikus

By Bryan Thao Worra

Sandalwood city
The moon hangs high above us
Night fragrant and calm.

So many temples here,
Monuments and kind people
The Buddha strolls by.

See the Talaat Sao,
How the Morning Market grew.
We trade first moments.

Quiet history,
Pristine Eden, paradise
Between civil wars.

Climb the Patuxai
Honoring veterans here:
An arch, a fine view.

Doctors and nurses,
Old Mahosot Hospital.
Health and Sabaidees.

Mattie and Chris film
Ghost movies and other stories,
A sleepy whippet

No giant monsters
Have been seen here in ages
Oh, how they slumber!

My family left
Years ago, but, oh, memories,
Seeking each other.

If you come visit,
Have a BeerLao by the shore.
Dear Mekong, khop jhai.

Circle That Luang
Making merit, remembering
Those who came before.

When you depart home:
On the Wattay tarmac, wish,
And you might return.

WELLINGTON

The Topography of Wellington

By Jennifer Compton

There is a darkness here: and also an itinerant rainbow
strolling like a twister with one lazy finger dipped in water.
There is a harbour: because of the rainbow there may be
a glory, like a saint's halo, which is an optical effect. Glory.

There are six kereru in Orangi-Kaupapa Rd feeding on miro:
or puriru,tawa, tairare. These birds are almost too indolent
to fly, the telephone wires zig-zag under their exiguous feet.
As they pause - in their top heavy survey of topography, let

us consider our understanding of living above. Above contains
below. Look up to the hills and sky, look down the way a river
runs. You are having it both ways now. The sun seeks you out.
In the deep of night before dawn the wind and the rain blow in.

Look down into this glittering city, high on your slippery hill and
shrug. Would they have called it View Rd if it didn't have a view?

YEREVAN

Yerevan Nights

By Lola Koundakjian

I curse that word
Its idea
The owner of that bar.

I spit at the face of its creator
The patron
The singer
In general, the drinker.

In my dreams, I am on a bed of clouds
Reclining
Reposing.

The smell ofcoffee
The woodfire
The dark
The C/A/L/M

—*Translated from Armenian by* the author

EUROPE
EVROPA

AMSTERDAM

The Dockhand

By Joris Lentra

He's got a mouth like a river, juicy and toothless.
Everybody loves him because he's willing to shoulder anything
Without ever complaining.
He shifts tons through small waterways to Germany.
What kind of region would it be without him here? Farmland?
He can bestow titles, like a king can.
But if you think you can rely on him,
The wind is tranquil, the surface playing dolphins,
Ships floating smoothly towards their dock,
He calmly surprises you from under his cap:
'Do you know that joke about the water that took the waterway?'
Well, then we turn dead pale:
That joke is not at all funny!
You can see how, on his turbulent banks
We've erected temples to Health and Wealth,
You can hear us behind the levee, chanting like shamans:
'Maas City, Maas County, Maas Theater.'

ANDORRA LA VELLA

Andorra: The Voice of the Mountain

By Ester Fenoll Garcia

I open my eyes
fine snowflakes
blanket Andorra

I tirelessly stroll
through wild woods
that fill my life with peace

the key
that unlocks the world to me
is hidden safely in these mountains

buried next to
the deepest roots
asleep with my oldest secrets

the sky and lakes
guard the silence of dawn
a bird undertakes its first flight

murmuring of water
gathers momentum
mirroring the blue

when snow will melt
in the month of May
it will be the season of daffodils.

ATHENS

Big Heat

By Claire Askew

'If I move now, the sun
naked between the trees
will melt me as I lie.'
—Adrienne Rich

Because I am the one who speaks English,
they call me outside.
In the street, in an elbow of weak light
thrown by our porch, two tourists
mumble like fat, white grubs.
The boy comes up the steps to me,
hand round a bad map someone drew.
His face is hot, red, wet as a tongue.
The girl is crying. They are looking
for a house that, when they find it,
will be shuttered, lime-scale white
and dry. I want to say
that crying is a stupid luxury
the local women can't afford:
I trained my babies early
not to dehydrate themselves this way.
I know it will be morning now
before this girl, her massive backpack
full of useless things, can find
the market, buy a quart
and pull that water back
inside herself again. But I'm quiet,
pour a glassful for her from our fridge.
She sputters *thank you* in our language.
Things that thrive here: mules

and stones, crickets loud as fire alarms,
the harder vines. Old women
whose hands and feet are tough,
whose men worked boats or built homes
all day in the big heat,
and died young. The boring sun.
Slow flies the size of grapes.
My father finds the torch and guides them
down the street's steep shoulder,
holding the light down round their feet,
until they are out of sight.
All night, under the chattering fans,
I think about the girl's chapped throat,
the boy she lies beside,
their mouths. None of us sleeps.

ATHENS

Athens-Thessaloniki-Istanbul

By Katerina Iliopoulou

There is this statue in the city
Which nightly treads on people's dreams.
Its marble fingers
Separate the entwined bodies
Some it touches on the forehead
And some on the lips
Planting a hook inside the hearts of others.

But people know nothing of this.
They all love the statue dearly
Every so often they crown it with flowers
They leave relics and mementos by its side
At other times they passionately cover it with kisses
On its hands, eyes and feet.

And on its flesh they inscribe their most precious secrets
Names and places they have been
And even, sometimes, poems.

—*Translated by* Konstantine Matsoukas

BELGRADE

The Old People in Our Street

By Jelena Lengold

The old people in our street
walk in the park every day
staking their life with their cane
like leaves.
Sometimes they stake through the heart
of a young green leaf
which utters a moan.
The old people don't care about this
and say that they are deaf.
And so from one bench to the next
they wave, stake,
and drive birds and bees away
complain about the air and the sun
criticise the wind
warn the shadow to get out of their way
they nag the world for revolving
without anyone even asking them
in which direction and till when.

BELGRADE

Belgrade

By Milan Dobricic

The smell of linden-trees
a tremor of water
the scuttling of sparrow
the limping of pigeons
the whistling of ships trains trucks
The diseased market-place myrrh
Drunkenness
Midnight of the streetcar variety
Unsung

—*Translated by* Novica Petrović

BERLIN

Berlin Now As Then

By Hatto Fischer

That was not what I had expected to see, Berlin at the end of the bar, mind you the Einstein café was created by an architect friend from Hamburg, and who went to Paris for the materials to cover the seats and sofas, while the carpenter of this longest bar had already fitted out Onassis' yacht. It meant simply the old-new capital after reunification in 1989 undertook by the stretch of the imagination something to refine itself, after all there were bunkers and rest of the wall to be overcome like big shadows outdistancing any light to be cast upon the new Chancellery and the extended parliament buildings huddled next to Brandenburg gate and the waves of stones called Holocaust memorial.

Underneath new tunnels unified all the train stations – there used to be four, and were called the iron lungs pumping in and out two million people or more flocking over the weekend to the outskirts of Berlin, while crowding on boulevards and squares like Unter den Linden and Potsdamer Platz, but which said nothing to the West when the wall stood to divide and to separate what belonged really together, not since centuries but when Berlin was built up rapidly in 1871 onwards to become a city with many housing estates that stretched way back into court yards leaving those on the lower floors with hardly any light, while everything, including dust went up but four floors: Staub Hoch Vier! It is a matter of measure, when you seek to grasp the diversity of a city and meet only conformity: same staircase, same cuts of apartments, and all windows directed towards the inner courtyard with the fire wall making sure no one could look out in any other direction, since there stood the other house.

A boy was selling at the crack of dawn his newspapers. The father, a butcher, stood at a distance to keep an eye on what

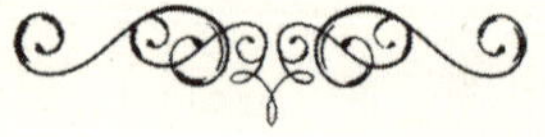

was going on. There was not much traffic around that time, but a limousine stopped and a boy out of his class rolled down the window to ask him for a newspaper. Money was handed over, a few words exchanged, and then the limousine drove off again. Something like that people of Berlin feel with all the dignities who have returned from Bonn and elsewhere to reoccupy the villas at the edge of Tiergarten, and with them politics rolls on like intercity trains leaving aside all small villages and towns and even stretches of land not known for anything but a boring life, while everything, so it is assumed, happens in Berlin.

BERN

Bern

By Brigitte Fuchs

What does the old bear bidden say to me?
Legend he is, a prolific heraldic animal.

Since he lent the city its name, he holds
the Berner (clumsy and unhurried) on his toes.

In the morning he rises from the Bear Park
to the Nydeggbrücke and into the soft round bow
of the Aare, as he observes the Swiss
Federal Council venturing a sevenfold guess.

He likes to present himself as a talisman before
the popular Zytgloggeturm, the sound of the
Glockenspiel in the left ear, mixing (mostly
unrecognized) with people mingling at the
Zibelemärit and poses as a bear cub
with scale shotgun to protect the fountain trough.

Mid days he peacefully climbs the medieval Münster
or strolls the arcades from honey bread to honey roast.

It was not always pure honey licking in Bern,
he says, the rascal, and retreats while dancing
on two bear paws into his winter-proof cave.

—*Translated by* Basil Fuchs

BRATISLAVA

Bratislava

By Mary Jo Salter

So I'm still alive and now I'm in Bratislava.
That's funny. I hadn't expected to be alive.
A sign in italics nudges us at the station:
Have an amazing time in Bratislava!
That's funny: a straight-faced wish, offered in English
and then Slovakian, posted above a trash can
that stands like the only monument in town.
We've heard there's a castle, though. We need a tram.
We take one, and it heads in the wrong direction.
A pretty girl, cheerful and blonde, straightens us out,
and we get on and off a bus at the proper stops.
That's funny. Already a right place and a wrong one
to be in Bratislava, and I am among
the people who sort of get this, at least at the moment
I happen to occupy, within a vacation
in Vienna with a day trip to Bratislava.
That's funny. I'd assumed my travel companion
through life would be my husband, even if
I'd gone to Bratislava, which I hadn't thought of
long enough to think I would or wouldn't.
The spanking white castle, standing high on a hill
we climb on foot, swigging our bottles of Coke,
dates to the year eight hundred or so, but burned
down to the ground, which tends, as we know, to happen,
and was reconceived in one of the worst times of all,
the 1950's, under Soviet rule.
That's funny. Atop embarrassing pillars, knights
in plaster armor gaze up at the sky
triumphantly, although what for is forgotten,
and the sunlight they eclipse in silhouette

is all the sillier on those phallic cannons
between their legs, with three or four cannon balls.
More cannon balls per man. That's human history
in a nutshell. Bullies unsated with all they've got
and below, the blindsided masses. That's what it is.
And yet I'm happy, now, with my companion—
he likes me, I like him. He has his own back story
of bleak encampments, battles lost, and sorrows
best not spoken of in Bratislava
lest we spoil our day, which so far is duly amazing.
I admire his dignity. Dignity is funny.
Everything's funny now, which we hadn't expected
to happen, either of us, after what happened.
We're still alive and now we're in Bratislava.

BRUSSELS

Charles Baudelaire in Brussels

By Willem Roggeman

With a burning suitcase full of melancholy
Baudelaire leaves for Brussels April 24th 1864
in order to escape his creditors
and in the hope of finding a publisher
for all of his poems which he sees
exploding at every corner of the street.
He dreams of a black goddess
in a room at the Hôtel du Grand Miroir,
28 rue de la Montagne, whose inner courtyard
is decorated with a golden fountain gushing out time.

The hell of his memory takes him back
to the time of his journey to Calcutta
where he almost dissolved
into the realms of death,
before he had gone past the Ile Maurice.

A spine-chilling instinct haunts him
like dreams under a tropical wind
and gentle reproaches resound from his bed.

The poet wants to flee but hangs on to his image
in the mirror. His soul is only rain.
A lake forms in the depths of his eyes.
Five fingers drop from each hand.

In a fervent moment he discovers
the artificial paradise of hashish.
He thrusts a dagger at the night,
remains blinded by his own light.

He tears at his own body
to make words that fly through the sky.

He traverses imaginary streets,
touches the consciousness of the early morning,
evokes the perfume of dreamt-up women,
distractedly caresses the ebony of his mistress.
Meanwhile, the town crackles in his fingers.

Porte de Namur he walks slowly,
with a dandified, almost feminine, gait
on a slope of the ground.
With his brilliant white collar he appears
at once clergymen and actor.
On the tip of his patent-leather shoes
he jumps elegantly over the puddles.
He is reflected in all the shop windows
and searches for evil in the accursed words
which like flowers open on to the paper.

He draws a diagonal line through suffering,
invents the beauty of prostitution,
of the wrinkled skins of old women,
who have suffered much from their lovers,
their children or through their own fault.

His body, wracked by syphilis,
bears the patina of strange demons
such as paralyses and problems of speech.
When his memories have paled,
his face is deconstructed in a lighted shop window
and becomes a drawing by Matisse.

The town yelps behind the faded facades,
reveals another perspective on misery.
How sadly sings decline in the badly-lit room
where the solitary poet lies amidst empty bottles

and thinks of the cruel creole, Jeanne Duval,
she of the gentle black breasts,
the deaf sources of her sadness.
He strokes the beauty of her scars
and becomes the dearest friend of her shadow.

At the church of Saint Loup de Namur
he sees his friend Félicien Rops blurr
and disappear into the rustling of the night.
He dies in the arms of his mother
who never understood him.

In Montparnasse, one sometimes hears him
still groaning and swearing in his tomb.
And each time a wild flower rises,
it utters the new name of evil.

—*Translated from the Dutch by* Susan and Roy Eales

BUCHAREST

In Cismuigi Park

By Astrid Alben

Ioana Ieronim sits cross-legged on the bench.
'The Chinese had Flaubert, Stendhal, and, of course, Rimbaud.
In Romania we read *1984*, *The Mark on the Wall*,
had Ziggy Stardust blue stacked to our bedroom wall.'
Ioana whips out a plasticised clipping from her skin-tight jeans.
Much like flashing ID.
Here are husband and a wife, side by side,
in front of a factory wall.
The Ceausescus are curtseying, rising to their feet – bowing
out of time, rising to their feet – bowing out,
their backs to the future, knees buckled:
this is the second the shutter shut,
the caesura where they are shot.
Yet here they are, buckling all this time.
Helena in camel coat and a 70s Floral Rayon blouse
is a housewife made of leavened bread and pickled sardines.
I look away.
The horror of tyrannicide lies in its intimacy.
The wooden oars of the rowboats splashed across the lake.
I look at my hands.
Scratch & pop the healing blisters on my foot.
I look at Ioana's mouth mouthing the names
of those that survived: Valentin their son (a scientist
at the Institute of Atomic Physics), most of the Party,
the balcony from where they bankrupted the crowd,
aunt Brandusa, the port Ioana Ieronim.
It's always the others that die, she says,
history comes at a cost, I mean, she says, just look at us.
This then is the trauma of Romania, she says:
resignation and its bitter resilience.

I return years later,
wrecked,
dismal, ailing with glory
and whatever else I recall.
I was young here, when democracy was young.
Then I got old before I got young.
Distant voices hum along arthritic electricity poles.
Ravens lick their scabs.
In Cismuigi Park
I step away from the bench,
the heat quivering in the yellow grass,
the oars splashing on the lake,
from those two bodies about to hit the ground,
from falling leaves and I caught none,
from promises that nothing will ever change
in a way we won't recognise
and finally of a loved one who once told me
No Goodbyes Thanks.

BUDAPEST

On the Cadence of Forgetting

By Ágnes Lehóczky

For D.R.

'The only time I visited the city, many years ago, I was stuck in a hotel room in winter, sick and delirious, overlooking the Danube with vast blocks of ice floating down the river while Laura went out to try to find some pot noodles or dried soups from some garage still open. And so, having nothing else to do', she writes, 'I read'. The folio of fog. The final hours of the last day were oppressed by low-lying clouds in Franzstadt. The grey mist rose from the riverbed crawling above fin de siècle courtyards, via lichtofs to the tops of giant furnaces stripping the Market Hall of its coloured tiling, the firewalls of the Mills of their soft sepia. It haloed the silent Slaughterhouse, erasing the pigmentation of the Habsburg iron bridge (with its bronzed falcon long flown off). The trams, scanned, oxidised, exited time. The riverbank disappeared from the map removing every little black dog from along its public paths. The sun right above the bridge died out like a gas ring, the way those pale inhabitants, unnotified flâneurs also slowly bled away in a phantom Europe. The old year's unpublished account of what had occurred in the here and now before. This, you could call, a new year's resolution.

Post Scriptum on Snow and Cactus

The Christmas cactus flowered overnight. Magenta was just everywhere. Cracks in the walls got a thumb wider. But, the architect warns, you are safe, the sky won't fall down. Unnameable street is scaffolded securely on the world atlas. No such thing as fissure between the thought and the said. In the fibre of fears. Codices are delicate. Skin survives apocalypses caused by a

turning page. Tonight winter has solsticed in the city. And snow just everywhere. All elements carry the same heavy fog weight, tons of ash. Study the consequence of the falling snow. What each breath, too, becomes. Say you could live with the mind of an hourglass, a tunnel engineer's thinking, the convex and concave form of being here & there. An old snow-plough sweeps across the winter evening. Creaking like old wars. You could always withdraw yourself from the map and once more, in a whiteout, become. You might go so far as to call it the sovereignty of saying, an unwanted one, but one, nonetheless.

BUDAPEST

Reel
By George Szirtes

For Clarissa Upchurch

1.

You wake to car sounds, radios, the cold sunlight
Burning holes in windows, and you sense
The missing fabric of the previous night.

The city offers you no evidence
Except the collage of the overheard,
Extended clauses of a broken sentence

Of which you recognise the odd stray word.
A car door slams. Feet scutter down the stairs.
It is the Theatre of the Absurd,

A masquerade in which the company wears
Period dress, their every movement fragile,
Negotiating brittle stools and chairs.

Eclectic, Art Deco, Secession style
Buildings multiply into a capital
Of iron, bronze, glass brick, ceramic tile.

A statue balanced on a pedestal
Is leaning over to whisper a close secret.
Two yellow trams clatter in mechanical

Circles. Dull monuments express regret
For what someone has done to them, for crimes
Committed in names they're trying to forget

But can't. Here all the clocks tell different times.
All the statues point different ways. Film crews
Shoot Budapest for Berlin. The city rhymes

With its imperial neighbour, like one bruise
With another. People converge on streets
Where there is never any lack of news.

Here is a square where everybody meets.
Here is a doorway through which troops have pressed.
Here is a yard with women hanging sheets
And corridors where boys in Sunday best
Are waiting for a housekeeper or maid
To join them on a stroll in the soft west

Wind ruffling the embankment trees. Decade
After decade resolves itself in the traffic.
The filming goes on somewhere in the shade.

2.
Once you arrive in the heart of the exotic,
Which is only a transferred idea of home,
Under the crumbling stucco, the faint brick

Of memory appears. Above the lanterned dome
Of the cathedral the familiar sky
Waves back, reflected in the brilliant chrome

Of legions of saloon cars purring by.
It is as if they drove some narrative
Whose visual sub-plot struck your painter's eye

With its peculiar imperative.
Even the light here has grown eloquent,
Its language sparklingly authoritative.

The city glories in its element.

I woke here as a child once in a narrow
Bedroom that served as my Old Testament.

Like a philosopher I watched Time's arrow
Winging towards its target and falling short.
So God is said to note a falling sparrow...

Genesis, Exodus... it was a fishing port,
An English holiday town, time blew me to,
Where I could watch waves, like immortals, sport

With bits of flotsam once the wind was through.
Here I find lost bits of my heart. In these
Dark corridors and courtyards something true

Survives in such obsessive images
As understand the curtains of the soul
Drawing together in the frozen breeze.

And you, born in the Far East, in a bowl
Of China dust, carried in armoured trucks
Along Malaysian roads, and down the coal-

Seamed valleys of Yorkshire, past viaducts
And airports, can now enter through the walls
To haunt the darkest residential blocks.

3.
What hope for rhyme when even childhood calls
On fiction for an echo and completes
Itself in myths, processions, carnivals,

Displays that billow down mysterious streets?
The city is unfixed, its formal maps
Are mere mnenomics where each shape repeats

Its name before some ultimate collapse.

The train shunts in the sidings, cars pull in
By doorways, move off, disappear in gaps

Between the shops. It is like watching skin
Crack and wrinkle. Old words: *Andrássy út*
And *Hal tér*. Naming of streets: *Tolbuhin,*

Münnich... the distant smell of rotting fruit,
Old shredded documents in blackened piles,
Dead trees with squirrels snuffling at the root.

On balmy afternoons you walk for miles
Trying to listen to the architecture.
It mutters continually, waving dusty files

Of unsolved grievances. It wants to lecture
Even while it sings - and how it sings,
When the mood takes it! So you take its picture

And brood upon those mouths and eyes, the wings
Of its cracked angels and draw out the sound
In terms of light which darkens as it rings.

Bells of the city chime, round upon round.
The film rolls on. A car sweeeps round the bend,
Its shadow stripping grey from the pale ground.

CHIŞINĂU

Chişinău

By Marina Khlebnikova

Central Avenue, the axis of the old Chişinău.
One hundred steps away from there
the city turns into an intestinal volvulus,
a maze of dark back lanes with
single-storey houses.
The tin plate of a crippled lantern
swings so violently,
the street seems to sway along –
and they creak together.

—*Translated from the Russian by* Anatoly Kudryavitsky

CHIŞINĂU

Tendency Toward Vagrancy

By Phillip Nikolayev

I've long had what Soviet psychiatrists
called 'a tendency toward vagrancy.'
At four I would run away from home
repeatedly for a whole day, alone
or sometimes with an accomplice named Boris
of like age. We knew full well we 'just can't do this,'
but nudge for nudge and wink for wink,
we'd board the trolleybus #10, I think,
buy tickets at four kopeks each
from our gleanings and savings of the week,
stick them into the ticket punch on the wall,
watch the chad fall as you pulled,
and ride all across Chișinău in half an hour
to get off near that unforgettable restaurant
built in the likeness of a huge wine barrel.
We peered inside, it was cool.

Then we had options:
go and splash in the local artificial lake
(I couldn't swim yet),
wonder in between along the banks,
catching frogs to take home in a glass jar
to populate a small construction pond (why
did we always use *my* shirt to do this?),
or go and explore the local flea market,
which was not at all safe to do,
but even at four it's nice to have options.
(One guy sold what we thought was a gun,
we asked him and he confirmed it.)

Those were days of cholera epidemics
in Moldova. We'd buy peasant-cooked
fodder corn on the cob when we got hungry,
haggled with old ladies over pennies.
We wouldn't catch the return trolley until sunset.

Then it's always the same picture:
the wicket creaks open, the landlord's mutant
barks through froth, my wet shirt clings,
I step out of the dark
toward my mother waiting by the door
of our 'temporary house' on Kaluga Street,
which was a bit of a dirt road, probably still is.
She has been crying, takes me inside.

Room and kitchen (no bathroom
or running water); the room
had a brick stove, the kitchen
a dirt floor (with mice and sometimes grass)
and a white washstand — these lines
are all that has survived of them.
There was great beauty in their squalor.

She has been crying, takes me inside,
says she will scold me later.
I know it will be soon. First she must call
the cops to tell them I've been found.
Of course, back then I didn't understand anything:
neither how a poet harms his mother,
nor how alienated (thank you, Marx, for that term)
one can be from the start, and free
in the grip of that greatest paradox of all —
a happy Soviet childhood.

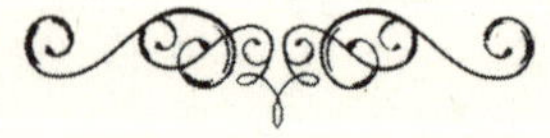

COPENHAGEN

Copenhagen

By Philip McDonagh

At Horsholm, Holte, and along the coast
the subfusc autumn colours of the trees;
by every bus-stop workers at their post
before the dawn, in silent companies;

the unforced elegance of market squares
and royal roofs flushed greener by the rain
as mid-day shoppers scuttle to the lairs
of gleaming galleries chock with porcelain;

and Langelinie, where that northern belle
poised on her rock forever for the gaze
of passers-by, waits; us she cannot tell
of her lost love; no glance, no smile betrays

half-memories of the night which saw her trace
her careful kisses on a storm-drenched face.

In Domus Vista high above the town
we crumble pastry to the undertow
of still remembered songs; and looking down
on Fredericksberg – within, the quiet glow

of special candles, snow-lanterns; outside,
lamp-light brocaded on the dark duvet
of night – we will forget the loveless tide
where mermaids dwell, and one, poor fiancée

of nothing but her pain, whom passion's touch
turned – little mermaid, though your brave display

merits a pedestal, self-giving such
as yours, so prompt, distresses us; today,

a girl's her own; if lovely, knows her due;
to all that is expected of her, true.

COPENHAGEN

Immigrant in the City of the Little Mermaid

By Tabish Khair

It hurts to walk on new legs:
The curse of consonants, the wobble of vowels.

And you for whom I gave up a kingdom
Can never love that thing I was.

When you look into my past
You see
Only
Weeds and scales.

Once I had a voice.
Now I have legs.

Sometimes I wonder
Was it fair trade?

DUBLIN

Mullet Under O'Connell Bridge

By Gabriel Rosenstock

A group had gathered on Eden Quay
To watch the fish under the bridge.
A little fellow with a grey cap went by.
'Mullet!' says he,
'Fine weather for six weeks.'

And so it was.
The sun came out.
The same light shone
On Christ Church Cathedral
On Trinity College
On the Bank of Ireland
On a little shop boarded up
Where once keys were cut
And knives sharpened.

It searched for the remains
Of Viking and Gael
Shone on schools
On hospitals, on taverns and prisons,
On parks and houses and on the Zoo:
Monkeys there to welcome it with open arms.

The sun beamed down on cobbled streets
And alleyways
On the summer dresses of young women
On the Liffey
And on the fish –
That scarcely moved –
Mullet: they saw the future.

DUBLIN

Place Names, Dublin

By Pat Boran

(The name Dublin derives from the Irish *dubh linn,* meaning black pool)

Where the M50 crosses the M1
to join the N32
their car broke down, the classic
steaming open-bonnet scene,
with two or three, no four
kids in the back, wide-eyed
and frightened, darkness approaching,
the Sunday evening homebound traffic
a river in flood. I pulled up close
in front, walked back
along the verge to find
a couple dressed in full-length robes,
their cellphone dead, a map
on the dashboard folded
to the mess of veins and arteries
they sat there in, one road above,
another below, a third
spun out before them into empty space,
and cars and trucks and caravans
flung wide about them all
like satellites or stars,
in which confusion the names
I might have chanced meant little —
Clonshaugh or Collinstown,
Belmayne or Darndale —
all borders lost within the web of lights,
instead my finger homing in

on the black pool up ahead,
my voice, now foreign even to myself,
repeating: 'Don't worry now,
you're almost there.'

HELSINKI

Frame by Frame of a Suburban Winter Day in Helsinki

By Anni Sumari

[pre-morning]

snow falls in slow motion
someone wades into the dark
the unpronounced polar dawn is
quelled by snow sweepers and *sisu* spreaders

[morning]

still snowing, in slow motion
in the metro tomato-red,
the LCD forecasts -17 C, -18 C, -19 C, -4 C ...
the commuters do not communicate
the refugee baby in the pram looks stoic
the bad citizen who smells *pepsodent* is closemouthed
the good citizen who smells hangover is pensive
the baby boomer reads metro and calculates his remaining
working days
the generation-x listens to death metal on her personal stereo
the generation-y ponders her homework on her way to school
the generation-z kicks the walls of her mother's womb

[late morning]

darkness dims
quietude continues
enters the sun
the snow that sits on the fence melts faster

[afternoon]

no sound bite
no subtitle
things appear halcyon in the sun
the thrill of the child who sleds down
the snow-covered rubbish dump is short-lived
the youth skates on thick ice
the old lady trashes her leftover into the biodegradable bin
as she walks her finnish spitz to the dog park
exists the unassuming sun

[evening]
the stripped spruce
in the magnolia white desert gets more elegant
electric sauna opens door to the public
at the local, the restless debauchee, the remorseless divorcee
and
the blind date do not find a common subject
the juvenile and the senile gamble to lose
the beer can collector braves the cold to win
from the discomfort of their *suomi-soffas*,
the good old family watch ‘secret lives’ on their digital tv
after a meal of creamed potatoes
the naughty resists being shooed to bed
the dying lonely finally rests

[late evening]

the volume of taciturnity is turned down
the volume of darkness is turned up
the volume of alcohol rises in her blood
how does a blonde know it’s winter
everyone loves a fair hair joke by a fair hair
by the time both the karaoke rocker and the billiard shooter
miscue,
the boisterous goes home, still talking to himself

as soon as a blink of blackout signals 'last orders'
the vociferous hugs the security lady good night

[night]

what a freeze!
no sign of life
but for the snow fox,
the sexed and
the sleepless

KIEV

Bonfire Night, Kiev

By Anatoly Kudryavitsky

Tonight's blood moon,
a gaping wound in the sky.
The city has been running
a high fever: buildings swollen,
all the corners rounded.
Who was the last person to see
the cathedral and the television tower,
the favourite toys of a civilisation of choice?
Hands and chestnut trees
smell of bread.
We are the babies of the cause,
and we know the big belly
from the inside.
In an ancient chapel, a wall fresco shows
a naked man amidst elks and buffaloes.
Tourists – *Europe in ten days* –
want to know what century
that picture is typical for.

LISBON

Lisbon Not Lisbon

By Xavier Frias Conde

almond trees
are banned to meet fados secretly
while the last traces of the Atlantic
are sold in the black market
and old tramways are forced
to learn absences by heart

tonight Lisbon
wanders barefoot

no one plays fado
and there is
no trace of you tonight
along the banks of the Tagus

LJUBLJANA

An Apple

By Lucija Stupica

It is time for an apple, it is time to go
to the marketplace, as I used to move down
into the orchard to choose and pluck one myself
still in the morning, washed in dew.
It is also morning by the river cutting through it snake-like,
Babel is waking up, cutting through it snake-like,
I move down as if along a naked body,
smoothly and quickly, then one needs to stop,
to have a look, to choose, to bite so the lips
bleed youthfully fresh again.
I drink up the juice from the face,
I share out eyes and wounds,
everything is put in order:
eyesight and life and the tree,
with a blessing I split up the fruit
and I bite into it again,
and it is the town that bites,
and it is you who bite.

—*Translated by* Andrej Pleterski

LONDON

Mine The Gap

By Les Wicks

1. *London Ticket*

Burnin' and Luton.
Double deckers, (grumbled thrum) they outnumber
furtively immobile cars that stand out like
bermuda shorts as this simmered commute falls in a line.

Shy eyes on the opposite seat.
Everyone's talking the new
hoodie happy slap, kid in school uniform talking –
some geezer deep asleep on the #56
POW! Open handed and all a
mobile uplink, web pages showing
right lippy bitches their struck-up faces
as the whack cracks.
You see those hoodies wif phone man me
eever run or fight back no regrets
a Happy Kicking from me man for this is
RIGHT OUT OF ORDER!

London, tattooed with arrival -
trains like duressed armour, devastating when failed.
Long-distance buses are a sort of death
every bodily function closes down in an odoriferous,
slumped shuffle.
Air travel is the same, but with cortisone.
Dyke against wood, episodic rose.
Wavelets of waste, the empty corpse in equality.
British steam power. Commonwealth,
scars and bloody expertise.

LONDON

Story of a City

By Moniza Alvi

I could tell you the story of a city –
how I seduced it in the afternoon.
The silenced birds were tangled in its hair.

I tried to stroke its million arms, its domes,
swept of some dust and sweetened it with rain,
unwound the suffocating scarves of dirt,

Pounded it like a drum, like carnival time,
watched it stretch until it burst
with rhythm, paint and revelry and song.

Calming the city, subduing it my house,
I thought I'd store it high up on a shelf,
or slip it in my pocket like a pen.

I begged on its behalf – a coin, a stroke of luck –
then left it in the dark recesses of a shop
steadily receding to another continent,

retrieved its deserts, chasms, embryos,
its open squares and theatre steps,
observed its networks running in my hands.

I started to examine how it seemed to be
just stuffed and stuffed inside itself.
Though once I cracked it open like an egg –

heard the river roaming free, the named
and nameless threats, the interlocking worlds.
At night I lie with this uncharted city.

It turns to me and murmurs in its sleep
I need you. Make of me what you can –
my suburbs of ideas, my flames, my empty spaces.

LONDON

On Reading Sebastian Barker's the Land of Gold

By Todd Swift

1.
In mid-March, the sun rarely decides
to rise so hot before Easter to defend
gardens that light defines. Regicide
requires darkness; this I know, to unbend
so our vast London Sunday donates
surprising sun-fed August, boldly,
as a child throwing matches at a flower.
Our noon of wife and husband seized
suddenly, burnt tenderly in its hour by
a completed generosity that once held power

2.
by its arms on the moon-cold tree. Thank God
for all the blossoming white I see; forgive
me for hating the body Christened Todd.
My soul is not infertile though I was unseeded
from jolted birth, early as this spring
exploding from the earth. The calendar's insane.
Creative gifts are violent good instabilities.
Told to hide pain, better to show off styles
of disability, as deeper compensations, wild
gold lunacies, tossed arcwise from a flying

3.
train. This old-fashioned praise is stirred reading
poetry by the dead - friend Sebastian – lines
unfolding as if dying was how wine was poured –
ink spread green bright and glowing on paper

right as bread. It is never too late to be inspired
by light breaking into an England whose fair share
of it is portioned by a carelessly austere hand – rain
our daily ration. If I turn now to new romance
as sun abounds about our recreation grounds, blame
islands, clouds, yet allow a poem to sound

4.

as in the heart poetry still sounds on yellow days
of uncompromising, archaic, impassioned praise.

LUXEMBOURG

The White Dust

By Jean Portante

sometimes when a storm passed
water entered the door
escaping light,
soaking darkness
she advanced to perishables
and stopped
between salt and flour
in hesitation of the whiteness
water only knew her worth
when flames were made
in high furnaces

a special alchemy
ruled over the flow of substances
redness transformed into greyness
it rained white dust on the city
it was flouring memories
salting those who had to be forgotten

all the furnaces are put out now
but the storm still passes
water entering the door sparkles
sometimes it is red

this redness — I know it's worth
when the blood passes in veins
and advances to perishables
and stops in hesitation
between salt and flour

—*Translated from French by* Elizabeth Tulatova
and Christopher Macann

MADRID

Madrid

By Germain Droogenbroodt

Don't envy the elder kingdoms nor its treasures:
the Alhambra of Granada,
the mosque of Córdoba,
the Rio Grande of Sevilla
nor the splendid paintings of el Greco in Toledo.
Be what you are now:
the cultural centre of the Iberian Peninsula.

MINSK

'How Hard It Is To Pull Ourselves Up...'

By Valzhyna Mort

How hard it is to pull ourselves up
from the pose of a question mark
into the pose of an exclamation.
The left labia of Poland and the right labia of Russia part
and our heads emerge out of
what?
By now we have sixteen names for snow –
it's time to come up with sixteen names for nothing.

In the pose of a question mark –
with our whole bodies we call ourselves into question,
confirmed by a dot of urine.
Is it us? Really? Calling into a question?
Or adolescence has just birthed
a rumpled beach towel.

So blunt were
the midwife's scissors
that with time they turned into
brightly-polished avenues
jointed by a military obelisk.
A tractor plant started manufacturing hair-rollers,
and every Sunday they sent mother
a gift basket.
Her head in rollers –
the ideal reconstruction of the solar system –
was photographed for albums and calendars.
The principle of rollers clenching hair
underlay the national production of harvesters.
This became my first metaphor

which I gobbled till my mouth foamed
as if I had swallowed the whole Swan Lake.

My body didn't belong to me.
Bent with pain,
it was making a career out of being a question mark
in the corporation of language.

The bureaucracy of the body drove me to the wall:
head didn't want to think –
    let the eyes watch
eyes didn't want to watch –
    let the ears listen
ears didn't want to listen –
    let the nose smell
nose didn't want to smell –
    let the hands touch
the body blooming with linden flowers of pain.

Where are my bees?
Aren't I sweet enough for them?

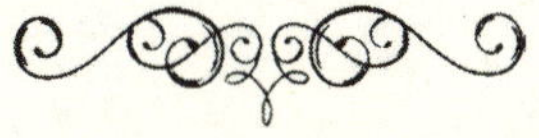

MONACO

Monaco

By Abhilash Surendran

After visiting the French Riviera
I headed east, closer to Italy
there was so much money in the air
nothing else that I could see

but Lamborghinis
plying on the road
and brand new swanky vessels
dotting the ocean line

amidst so much of affluence
I felt lonely
like a fly on the wall
glued to money.

MOSCOW

Moscow, 1990s

By Phillip Nikolayev

White chains of snow over the city's limbs
distract the crows. Black slush is full of fire.
Impervious to the wind, a Volga climbs
uphill with taut tenacity of tire,
slowing at icy places. In twilight
a few scattered pedestrians stomp and steam,
rubbing their ears red in a sprinted flight
to the Metro from a capitalist canteen.
The parks begin to yawn, where statues still
stand half-emphatically, as if leaning
toward the vacuum of a lost empire.
Large are the workings of the general will,
but in the early February evening
Moscow's true stars are menacingly clear.

NICOSIA

Jasmine

By Nora Nadjarian

She reached the line:
the perfume, the white scent
leading her. Jasmine.

It was her childhood again,
visiting; like that small breath
of flowers from another's garden

as she passed by, a child playing
the fence railings like the harp.
Come, come, the scent pulled her,

Always. But the garden was not hers,
she was told. Nor was the aroma,
which lured and dared her to trespass.

Now, as she crossed the un-straight,
the invisible, the impenetrable line,
and as the blue-bereted soldier

watched her feet closely, eye-measuring
the millimetres, and as his mouth
opened to call out HALT!

she was a child again, running, strong.
HALT! they called but she didn't turn.
Furious pages were missing in the book

of her life. And, breathless, she thought
of the jasmine she was to find; the house
she was to see; the garden; the fence;

and her father's buried heart.

OSLO

There is No Wind in Oslo

By Mark Strand

‘My dear’, said the traveler to the young woman,
‘life has not been kind to me; I went north in
search of the famous Alaskan pigmy dog but never
saw one; I went south to catch a glimpse of the
long-tailed, blue-green African rhino and failed
again. Inconsolable, I gave myself to the sullen
glory of great poems and ended up here, on the
windiest corner of the windy city.’ ‘Go to Oslo’,
said the young woman, ‘there is no wind in Oslo.’

PARIS

Stranger in Paris

By Michael Glover

It is columnar, and entirely made of ice.

I cannot run away from it fast enough –
 the swifter I go, the sooner I arrive.

There is no speech in its mouth –
 merely the faint washings of bad breath.

The whole of it falls on top of me at all times.
That is why I must stay still beneath this bed.

I blow its name out into the air. It forms into
large and unwieldy chunks of volcanic rock.

If I were to collect up all the spoons
from all the cafes, I would never walk.

If I were a trickle, I could merge
into its waters – those canals, that river,
the open sore of all its sewers.

I fling my windows wide – Rue des Augustins –
onto truth, righteousness, evil.
Everything is expanding on all sides...

Fine, grey pencil-strokes of rain fall slantwise
across the canvas of the sky, evasively.
Half of my face is wet – I may be crying.
The other half stays bone-dry.

In the courtyard below, six half-men circle
Two magnolia trees with wet, gleaming leaves,
Speaking in half-voices.
How can half-voices seem so fierce?

My words don't tell enough.
They shed their secrets sparingly.
Things get as far as the edge.
Then they draw back again.

There is nothing for me here.
My hands have become separated from my body.
My head lolls, as if thirsty for the basket.
Ask it. Ask it.

Paris, I say, *Paris, now come to me*.
Somewhere a blanket shifts, a train snorts.
Here is a brick. There – somewhere over there –
Is the sea. *Willingly*.

PARIS

My Father's City

By Pascale Petit

All of Paris is quiet, while the oxygen machine
struggles to fill your lungs.

The gargoyles' cheeks flush
from the strain of breathing for you.

The clouds are still – they won't
steal one minute from this morning.

Around the Périphérique, cars
switch off their engines. Plumes of vapour

rise from the streets where you lived –
rue de la Huchette, quai Saint-Michel.

Sparrows have nested in your doorframe,
it's so long since it was opened

and I have come to give you a bed-bath,
to shut the flowers in your skin.

The Jardin des Plantes locks its enclosures
as I dry the garden of your chest.

The winged ghouls of Notre-Dame crouch
on your shoulders as you sleep;

they have guarded the scar between your ribs
the last years of your confinement.

Their stone eyes stare at me
as I shake your arm. And when

car horns and sirens fail to wake you
and the doctor comes to switch off your oxygen,

I see you stretched on your narrow bed
like an etiolated city, O my father, all your gates closed.

PARIS

Visiting Paris

By Vijay Seshadri

They were in the scullery talking.
The meadow had to be sold to pay their riotous expenses;
then the woods by the river,
with its tangled banks and snags elbowing out of the water,
had to go; and then the summer house where they talked—
all that was left of an estate once so big
a man riding fast on a fast horse
couldn't cross it in a day. Genevieve. Hortense. Mémé.
The family's last born, whose pale name is inscribed on the rolls
of the Field of the Cloth of Gold. As in the fresco of the Virgin,
where the copper in the pigment oxidizes to trace a thin green
cicatrix
along a seam of Her red tunic,
a suspicion of one another furrowed their
consanguine, averted faces.
Why go anywhere at all when it rains like this,
when the trees are sloppy and hooded
and the foot sinks to the ankle in the muddy lane?
I didn't stay for the end of the conversation.
I was wanted in Paris. Paris, astounded by my splendor
and charmed by my excitable manner,
waited to open its arms to me.

PODGORICA

The Town Below the Hill

By Tanja Bakic

It's a city struggling between stillness and sound,
a city of peculiar routes and winding passages,
of whirlpools and scents from the sea.
There is too much light from sunshine here.
It starts early in the dawn. The city is then full of
shadows from the surrounding hills.
In old Podgorica,
water from the ancient fountains
drips off cobblestones
as an overheard song
at the houses built with white stones.
The historic Clock Tower
hearkens time bygone
and warped bridges
mirror themselves in flowing currents
of Ribnica and Morača.

— *Translated by* Gwen Charles and the author

PRAGUE

Today My City Dressed Up As a Warder

By Adam Borzic

Today my City is dressed up as a warder
In long flowing cloak, the color of rain
Seeks all fragile souls
And every time gives them the same frozen kiss
No one could escape its nervous constrict ring
No one could get round its poisonous fumes
And everyone and everything fell under the weight
Of its monotonous petting
Clerks today were powerfully present
In the air and laughing god Mercury
Directed each post office, tax returns
Rained on desks and secretaries in court shoes
Slept in queues, everything was so
Clogged, even sexy poetess
On television put on herself an apron
And wiped off kid´s mucus
From the nose, meanwhile
Lovers of America and Russia staggered
Because they were indistinguishable,
And threatened each other by invisible fists,
Just Mayor was well influenced by the air
Today say no shit.

My city, once I would like to
Put my head into your lap but I am afraid
You could tear off my head
And hang it on one of your magical gates
So I will be your poet only for tomorrow.

PRAGUE

Prague
By Khadijah Queen

Yes as thievery, except if saved for
a fantasy in which I in a backless
dress encounter

you on a typical balcony
overlooking Vltava, gripping the latticework,
metal, a barrier to leaping

into an esoteric night, fixed and ornate
enough, like my penchant for the infinite
within the singular, encounter you

as tributary, serpentine, the heat of your fingers
on my spine, my head turning
as you bend to catch the yes

I'd held latent, a mine you trigger with
your tongue, neither of us
mean to stop exploding.

REYKJAVIK

Bankastraeti Blues

By Claus Ankersen

Your legs of lamb, Reykjavik
the red, crispy, tender, juicy
young meat and the way you swim
like a fish in the water or round and around
a juniper bush
or a sushi counter
I drill my way under your skin, Reykjavik
peek through the crack of your fresh fillets
and walk in the white powder around your lakes
Up Bankastraeti
and back down
Up Bankastraeti
and down again on the other side
Up Banskastraeti and far out
into designer wilderness
along Laugavegur
and the vitaminized water, Reykjavik,
in all the colors of the rainbow
and the little elf children
with their clear eyes
on Nikitadurinn's tenth anniversary
I spot a glimpse of the old you
your unconquerable wind
your brutal snowfall
your sweet sun
the majesty of your mountains
It seems like you can't really make up your mind, Reykjavik
for winter hibernation or solstice rave
I think there is a monster
hiding beneath the quilted jacket, Reykjavik

a foodmonster
a drinkmonster
a dopemonster
Eat like a man, Reykjavik
fuck it and party through
After all, it's just Saturday six days a week.

RIGA

Postcard From Riga

By Irina Grivnina

Dragging along the grey
pavements between
the grey walls
seeing nothing around us
we only remembered
bad news
from home

The unkind icy rain
drove us into the lobby
of a deserted hotel
we found seats
by the huge window
outside which the grey river
was hitting against the stones
and
the cold city
gloomy and strange
looked us in the eyes

A sharp silhouette
seemed painted on the pale
Baltic sky -
the weathered and worn ghost
of the ancient grandeur
silvered with water drops

That bitter day
won't ever return
but the voice of

an old organ
by way of consolation
may call upon you
to walk the same route
along the grey pavements
between the grey walls...

—*Translated from the Russian by* Anatoly Kudryavitsky

ROME

Rome

By Luca Benassi

Rome is a box, a blue hive, with violet TVs glow,
carved in a row of red blocks, facing nights
squared by the buildings' heights. Concrete
has now conquered the sky
with marbles and scarlet columns
pushing away naked Gods,
their ancient spirits.

Rome is red sunsets
and golden days swept away from hills
with nothing left
but ruins that nurture a romance

unfathomable like a faint ray of light

Rome is a dwarf,
a language of despair
and endless circular flight of seagulls
getting drunk at the Emperor's dinner,
like a piglet stuffed with honey and apricots

Rome is an old woman's home
a garden of flowers of vivid colors
Rome is a big blue butterfly
love written secretly on her wings.

SAN MARINO

San Marino

By Abhay K.

Go to San Marino, someone told me in Torino. A country carved out of a mountain. The largest castle is still a prison. They say San Mario has the oldest constitution and has more vehicles than men.

SARAJEVO

Sarajevo Music
By Anatoly Kudryavitsky

The absence of bus
shines in the distance
(our dreams recall
what our days forget.)
The smell of peat fires
leads August into May
and further down the tunnel
of time.
Our train drags itself through the trill
of a pneumatic drill in the rain
(or is it a machine gun sound
chasing the echo of the whistle?)
As we wait for enlightenment
exactly where our travel map ends,
a boy wearing headphones
walks off the edge
into his silent music.

SARAJEVO

Sarajevo Sequence

By Sudeep Sen

1. Library

Footprint of the library of your childhood
is earth, soil and air now —

air is memory, memory photo-plates,
plates repository of translucent images

of fire, birth, and now — your time now.
When the library burned, it raged

for three days, and days and days after that
black snowflakes of ash stood suspended

in air. If you happened to catch one
on your palms, one could see actual type,

feel the lines, the italics slowly sloping off
their letter-form,

their serifs hiding narrative
within dark-grey sheathes of papyrus —

which only seconds later would break up,
brittle powder — ashed-paper residue.

Stories long forgotten, history erased,
memory blanched out in an accident.

2. Design

Black holes, power-grid towers,
cancer cells, bacteria corals —

centripetal questions of whether
'a brick wants to be an arch'

or Louis Kahn's wish for concrete;
dilemmas of design, grand design —

sparrow, ravens,
crows caught in mid-flight, arrested

as 'a spider weaves her web of light'
in looping parabolas of matt-nets —

endless lines of stringed pearls, jewels,
intestinal coils ending dragon-like

spouting, not fire, but coughs of ash.
'Fruit hangs heavy on the branches.'

'Heap it up and eat it, mangia,
let it stain your best blouse,' you plead.

Incarnadine Virginia creeper leaves —
insect-carved, craving — toned kudzu,

diaphanous grid of the rendition
of disappearance, a map, an orbital space

in which protons and neutrons spin,
clashing to make a new, old whole.

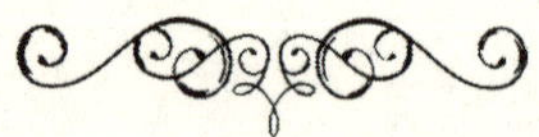

3. Ash

Two granite bowls, tipped askance,
        wearing ash-washed grey —

Velazquez talking to Vermeer
        perhaps, amphora

contain milk or paint or white ink,
        libation pouring out —

semen to reimagine lost memory,
        migrating cells to a new landscape.

Ash renews greys to browns to earth-colours —
        ruddy pastel autumn-tones —

a panorama containing within its folds
        passion, presumption, pre | text —

defying black and greys, the rainbow
        white, imploding into more white, white.

—triptych for Tanja Softic

SKOPJE

Lungs

By Magdalena Horvat

Skopje is cigarette smoke,
sky pierced by chimneys and factory towers,
all those cars exhausting—exhausted, like ours—
and it's had me so broken, so broke,

but I can breathe there because it's home.
I hate the smell, now that I no longer smoke,
but I can breathe. Despite the fake Baroque
facades, new monuments and domes,

the air is familiar. So are the songs.
The sounds. The traffic is frantic, and on the street,
nobody sees you, yet we're all friends, all family,
so eager to leave... Only then can we long

to go back: to breathe and teach our children
the language stuck in our throats, in our lungs.

SOFIA

The Travel Guide to the Country of Your Birth

By Kapka Kassabova

which
has over three hundred natural lakes
is one of the oldest countries in Europe
has something for everyone, in every season
occupies the northeast part of the Balkan Peninsula
sits on the Black Sea to the East
and the Danube to the North
offers white-sand beaches,
stunning mountains, and ancient towns
has the Balkan range,
which is part of the Alpine-Himalayan chain
has three hundred seventy eight kilometres of Black Sea coast.
The Black Sea is closed and non-tidal
and has no life below two hundred metres
has a moderate continental climate:
winters (November to February) are cold, dry and snowy,
temperatures reach minus ten
is the place where in dark, empty apartments
the people you love live inside mirrors

STOCKHOLM

In Stockholm

By Mathura (aka Margus Lattik)

When I was a boy, Stockholm
was a faraway place. I could only imagine
people strolling on the Drottninggatan,
checking into Domkyrka, sniffing the aroma
of the street cafés, or thumbing through
the rows of classics in a second-hand bookstore.
This was a world where winds were gentler,
the Sun brighter, where even air smelled better,
clear of the rust of the Iron Curtain.
This world is no longer.
Come and mount the Radisson with me now
and you'll see a dull dim line of ships
departing from the harbour,
not leaving but connecting.
Aren't maps created in the head?
Happiness, oh happiness, they say. Today
I stand at the National Gallery and, as
the Sun sets behind the window, I gaze
at Auguste Rodin's 'The Awakening of Man'.
It is nightfall in Stockholm. Stockholm is
beautiful. I am ordinary.

TALLINN

Tallinn

By Hasso Krull

It is dark, a few cars still passing like fireflies. The trees look medieval. A half-naked girl in golden shoes steps out on the street from a cellar. Somebody stops you: hey, do you have a lighter? You do. The flame evokes a face of a man out of the dark, a face like a snail spiraling towards the centre, a cigarette. Pointed spires. Is it true that they point towards another world, ilm, as they say in Estonian or used to say, when somebody lived up there? Old woman with head of ice, who never ate any human food, but only the roots of reed, seaweed and mud that she found on the shore at night. That heavenly shore... Then some wicked knights came and built towers sharp like a lance, to warn her not to come down.

Spires and darkness. You trot down the stairs and step into cellar bar like a vaulted cave. There was a girl who fled from her brother, she sat on the branch of an oak, just started to sing and the tree grew higher and higher. When it touched the sky she jumped down and went her own way.

Now she sits here in this bar, fingers touching the screen as she writes something into her phone. You peek: Facebook.

Oh it's raining in the street, on the cobblestones of another century and Tallinn sputters like a hedgehog on the coast of an ancient sea.

TIRANA

Early Evening, Downtown Tirana

By Morelle Smith

A new moon in the evening sky,
some blurs of pink above the squat horizon.
Some parts of the pavement
are completely broken up;
other parts are level, smooth new flagstones
set in careful cement, pink and green
and honey-coloured hexagons.
You tread carefully on them,
savouring their shape and colour,
their precise alignment,
through your soles.

On stone benches by the trees,
on wooden boxes outside shops,
men play dominoes and chess.
Dust rises in the potholed streets,
behind the cars.
The traffic rolls past slowly –
mostly long mustard Mercedes
or the white land-cruisers
of international relief teams –
Red Cross, UNHCR,
Médecins sans frontières
(dubbed *médecins sans voitures*
in the north, because so many
vehicles were stolen.)

Spring comes with a sudden
scent of flowers –
you can almost see Time loitering,

a hazy figure in the twilight,
streets strewn with stones and garbage
and an orange glow here and there,
from dying fires.

At night, when you walk
past the stadium
and the large van that is always parked there
with *première urgence* painted on its sides,
there is a small fire burning –
a few pieces of wood, red embers.
Sometimes there is someone squatting by the fire.
Often it just glows unattended,
by the railings,
underneath the trees.

VADUZ

In the Roundabout

By Mathias Ospelt

Should I go now to the 'Löwen'?
Or should I go now to 'Lett'?
Should I go to the movies?
Or should I go home to bed?

Should I drive to the Rheinpark Stadium?
Or should I drive now to Triesen?
Should I drive now to Rotenboden?
Or up to the Schaaner Wiesen?

Should I go on over now to Sevelen?
Or should I go now to Prättigau?
Should I go in the direction of Nenzinger Himmel?
Or even to Lustenau?

Should I drive out to Austria?
Should I drive out to Engadin?
Should I drive down to Lake Constance (Bodensee)
Or toTessin?

I could also just idle in this roundabout
Staying here wouldn't be so bad
Outside it's way too dangerous
Out there the world's gone mad.

VALETTA

Charlie, My True Love

By Immanuel Mifsud

A dog's turd in the middle of the street, crowned by a legion of flies. A couple of filthy strays wagging their tail. Two bars with empty tables: their jukeboxes in the middle of the one hundred year sleep, the spirit bottles standing straight. The barman smoking. He goes out spitting phlegm.

Welcome to the Capital.

September forces the sun to set earlier and from my neck emanates perfume. A coarse voice asks me, 'One cigarette please.' I have my *Dunhill* in the back pocket. 'Are you Maltese? Want to Come in honey? Hmm? Come have a drink. Don't you want, sweetie? Come on in let's have a Beer.'

A *Hop Leaf* ale in one hand while she ruffles my hair with the other, smiling at me with her eyes the colour of those flies in the middle of the street. She uncovers her breasts as soon as I enter. Like the Virgin Mary leaning against the wall with a candle burning – even she bares her breasts, and so does her son. No pillows on the bed. The side table. The dark. And downstairs the jukebox wakes: *Tainted Love*.

'Five pounds, sweetie.'

Thank God I raided my mother's wallet before going out. A tiny room, very tiny and dark with a dim light coming from a red candle lighting the Virgin's bosom and Jesus looking at me point at his chest: *oooh, look, what a crown of thorns you've thrusted in my heart. Look at the flame of my love.*

Tainted Love.

She teases me with her tongue and laughs and lies on her back with the second *Dunhill* between her lips.

In her chest there's no love. There's only the spittle of the guy who had gone there before me. And wrinkles. And *Charlie My True Love*, tattooed in dark green with red highlights from one tit to the other. And I find myself fondling *Love* with my right hand and I go down kissing *Charlie*, while she does her best not to belch the ale in my face. There's no heart in her chest, much less the fragrant roses the Virgin has around hers.

Sweat. Reeking of sweat. The pungent odour of the bed. The smell of the guy who had gone before me.

With the smoke of the third *Dunhill* blown straight in my face, she smiles as she throws the loo paper in a bin, and covers herself, and tells me she hopes to see me again soon. Downstairs the jukebox reads my thoughts, *Now I've got to run away, I've got to get away* and again my eyes rest on the spirits bottles standing straight, and on the strange step of the barman going out to spit phlegm and on the turd in the middle of the street getting nibbled by a legion of flies. My eyes rest on the other ladies sitting on wobbly stools, with their legs open wide, looking at me with a darkful gaze.

The signs at the bars bid me farewell as I hurry through the narrowness: *see how the falling darkness looked at you? It sees you walking, it spots you, it keeps on moving; following your footsteps in this street which once was a picture in colours as flashy as loud singers.*

There was a bar and a barman and a woman who took my *Dunhill* and five pounds I took from my mother, and a tiny room where there was the Virgin Mary and there was Jesus too. And

there was a jukebox that woke for my sake. There were other women sitting on stools. There was the dogshit.

There was I, pressed between the street walls, between the room walls, between her arms, between her breasts, between *Charlie* and *Love*. There was love, there was so much love.

VATICAN CITY

Vatican City Vision

By Pat Boran

Halfway across St Peter's Square, I dropped
the guidebook, pages scattered, and the words
came to me out of nowhere: 'We could tear it down.'

Barbarians inside the gate, we could tear down
this whole splendid city, this gilded confection, this stunning
insult to the poor, the queer, the fallen out of grace

and favour. We could clear the galleries for beds,
the endless corridors for mess-hall tables; we could serve
the homeless of the world in the black and white vestments

of these servants of the Lord. Then might we rid ourselves
of our dark obsession with power, with empire,
and with this palace for the millions at the heart of which
in his chains of faith the solitary prisoner endures.

VIENNA

Vienna

By Priya Sarukkai Chabria

A peephole, an iris closing on itself:
My view of Vienna or von Stroheim's shimmering
film of him playing his dream: the Count immaculate in debauchery.

Notice at entrance of early 20th century club:
'*Mistresses allowed only if they are wives of other members.*'
Vienna, what civilization had you dreamt?

10 pm, Innere Stadt.
Dark windows wear white lace vestments.
There's only so much one should know.

I'm an outside at home looking out:
City of Dreams – not Freud's but mine,
City of imperial moorings adrift as tourist tout. This too, you.

The Danube a silver shadow chasing itself, its pasts, its mouth.
Begin not with spring, but silt. Depositions, encrustations, memory
washing its banks: slit vein ermine fleeced within.

Palaces paintings portraits gleam in oily darkness clasped in gilt.
White lace froths on pleated white lace as the Empress grasps her fan. The Hapsburg
empire ends. Or does Maria Theresa's clutch continue in us as controlling will?

In my mouth melting Mozart Balls.
How many can one devour without sickening?
Chocolate, men, music: when is enough enough?

music music music music music music

Within a drift of snowflakes
eat steaming maroni near the Opera.
The round translucency of water chestnuts after Wagner's thick waterfall.

Museums

A room of flying carpets spills jewelled shades.
(*Relics strung from ceiling with invisible thread.*)
The threat of the Turks celebrated. This too is you, Vienna.

On view Durer's Hare. Queues
to see its crouched hairiness, its live eyes
leap into yours and shift art's gaze.

Velvet rooms of paintings. People part
for us to peer into Brueghels; we're from afar.
How beauty stalls- restores-vanquishes self.

Along the Ringstraße a park, a shallow stream
rippled by weeping willow reflections
flocked by herons.

The paraplegic on the other bank throws crumbs.
On both sides stream women pushing prams.
Time slips into stasis, collects.

Cakes coffee conversations
the last eavesdropped in tongue unknown.
Listen harder as if to hear a spider spin out gossamer.

Waltz to Grinzing for local wine: sparkling white light
streams in translucent leaves pale asparagus spears husband near
'…suddenly, like glory, it rests in the air.

But we don't know what to call it, we guess...
And the remembrance we build of those
hours of summoning doesn't capture it.'*

* *Sonnets to Orpheus by Rainer Maria Rilke translated from the German by David Need.*

VILNIUS

Calvaries

By Eugenijus Ališanka

a drunkard is flapping the air at the market place
his foul words from a sailor's bible
his spirit the resin of ebony
coagulates into sludge
on his shoes in the middle of the calvaries
all around the stations of stands
in the market cabbages are blooming again
a brat makes the sign of the cross and slips
his hand into my pocket
my blond little brother
once an altar-boy
when we broke watermelons like the host
in the middle of the yard
people are just people they will mill about
not thinking about sacred things, thank god
otherwise one wouldn't pass by these humps
these visors and masks, muslims, catholics
hare krishnas, vegetarians, but check out
that one in the middle, not even a hat for alms
how he is wailing and weeping
having taken my place

—*Translated by* Kerry Shawn Keys and Eugenijus Ališanka

WARSAW

Warsaw Redeemer

By Montserrat Villar González

Exiled from your actual time,
you raise your memories of grandeur
never destroyed
by collapses and shoots.

Expelled from your own roots,
you draw again your walls
ever surrendered to death
in your own arteries and shades.

I foresee while walking between your legs
the heaped stars, the left
coats coming up along the rails
that betrayed farewells.

However, I smile at you through that pain
still carried by the air. And the music
keeps on covering your squares and your streets
helping to forget omens of extermination,
and put birds of death off the corners
of this city that redeems us every morning.

ZAGREB

Fathers and Sons

By Tomica Bajsić

Standing by the ATM in the city where I was born
For the first time in my life I hold in my hand
the banknote of a thousand kunas with a portrait of Ante
Starčević,
called the father of our homeland Croatia.

I am clinging to it just for a little while,
before I enter the bank to pay the bills.
You are just like I imagined you to be, father,
your beard streaked with wisdom, eyes deep, inquisitive,
but you don't seem to be looking at your son with joy.
Surprised you are, but not happy at all.

It is me as I am, father,
Your son has grown old waiting in line
to meet you.

—*Translated by* the Author and Gabeba Baderoon

ACKNOWLEDGEMENTS

In this daunting endeavour, I have received support from poets across the world. They appreciated the concept of such a unique anthology, some wrote poems for it and many recommended poets who might contribute.

I want to deeply thank each contributing poet. Without their valued offerings it would not have seen the light of day. I want to thank each of the translators whose translations appear in this anthology. José Saramago reminds us that writers and poets create national literature but it is translators who create world literature. Let us salute our translators.

I am grateful to Kwame Dawes, Gabriel Rosenstock, Pat Boran, Hatto Fischer, Frank M. Chipasula, Anatoly Kudryavitsky, Ruth Padel, Christopher Merrill, Beverley Nambozo Nsengiyunva, Nikola Madzirov, David Shook and Ngwatilo Mawiyoo for their unstinting support in completing this anthology. I want to thank Rachana Mukhia for painfully going through the submissions and preparing the first draft of the anthology. I am grateful to Gary Ockenden and Deepa Velayutham for their valuable editing suggestions.

I want to thank artist Tarshito for contributing the cover image for this anthology, Pallavi and her team for designing the cover it graces, and Bina Sarkar Ellias for the perfect finishing touches.

I would like to thank Rajiv Beri, Paul Vinay Kumar, Jyoti Mehrotra, Raj Bilochan and Satyabrat Mishra of Bloomsbury India for their constant support and belief in this book.

I would like to thank Ekaterina and Kaya for their limitless patience, love, support and understanding during the completion of this labour of love.

I take full responsibility for any error that has inadvertently crept into the anthology. Thank you all.

PERMISSIONS ACKNOWLEDGMENTS

The poems included in the anthology have been voluntarily contributed by the poets and their translators. Permissions to include the poems listed below have been granted by the individual poets, translators and publishers. If, through inability to trace the present copyright owners, any copyright material is included for which permission has not specifically been sought, apologies are tendered in advance to proprietors and publishers concerned.

'Poems for Abuja' by Jumoke Verissimo from *I am memory* (Dada Books, Nigeria, 2008). Copyrignt © 2008 by Jumoke Verissimo. All rights reserved. Used by permission of Jumoke Verissimo.

'Algiers' by Christopher Merrill from *Imaginary Cities.* Copyright © by Christopher Merrill. All rights reserved. Used by permission of Christopher Merrill.

'Antananarivo' by Elizabeth Orlando from *A Field of Flowers: Poems and Essays from a Diplomat's Journey* (Xlibris, Corp. 2003). Copyrignt © 2003 by Elizabeth Orlando. All rights reserved. Used by permission of Elizabeth Orlando.

'Her Picture' by Ressom Haile from *Per Contra: The International Journal of the Arts, Literature and Ideas* (2005-2009). Copyrignt © 2005-2009 by Charles Cantalupo. All rights reserved. Used by permission of Charles Cantalupo.

'Bangui: Let the dust of the boots drown in Ubangi' *by Grandmaster Masese from pambazuka.org (Issue 718, 2015).* Copyrignt © 2015 by Grandmaster Masese. All rights reserved. Used by permission of Grandmaster Masese.

'Drumbeat at Night' by Tony Tcheka, translated by David Shook from the Portuguese. Copyright © 2013 by Tony Tcheka. Translation

Derek Walcott. All rights reserved. Used by permission of Derek Walcott.

'Poem for La Paz' by Carlos D. Mesa Gisbert, translation by David Shook from the Spanish original, Copyright © 2013 Carlos D. Mesa Gisbert https://carlosdmesa.com/ Translation Copyright © 2016 by David Shook. Used by permission of Carlos D. Mesa Gisbert and David Shook.

'The Recycle City' by Victoria Guerrero Peirano, Translation by Enrique Bernales from *Ya nadie incendia el mundo* (estruendo mudo, 2005). Copyright © 2005 by Victoria Guerrero Peirano. All rights reserved. Used by permission of Victoria Guerrero Peirano.

'Managua 6:30 P.M.' by Ernesto Cardenal, Translation by Jonathan Cohen from *Pluriverse: New and Selected Poems* (New Directions, 2009). Copyright © 2009 by Ernesto Cardenal. All rights reserved. Used by permission of Ernesto Cardenal and Jonathan Cohen.

'Night in the Gardens of Port of Spain' by Derek Walcott from *The Poetry of Derek Walcott, 1948-2013 selected by Glyn Maxwell* (UK by Faber & Faber, and U.S. by Farrar Straus & Giroux). Copyright © 2013 by Derek Walcott. All rights reserved. Used by permission of Derek Walcott.

'The Others' by Luis Chaves from *Chan Marshall*, 2005. Copyright © 2005 by Luis Chaves. All rights reserved. Used by permission of Luis Chaves.

'The Baku Wind' by Yeşim Ağaoğlu. Copyrignt © by Yeşim Ağaoğlu. All rights reserved. Used by permission of Yeşim Ağaoğlu.

'The Negative' by Arthur Sze, from The Redshifting Web: Poems 1970-1998. Copyright © 1998 by Arthur Sze. Reprinted with the permission of The Permissions Company, Inc., on behalf of Copper Canyon Press, www.coppercanyonpress.org.

'Facing East: a poem on the Aldeburgh memorial to Benjamin Britten and the City of Damascus' by Ruth Padel from *Learning to Make an Oud in Nazareth* (Chatto & Windus Radom House, 2014).

'In Jerusalem' by Mahmoud Darwish, from The Butterfly's Burden, translated by Fady Joudah.

'Manila to Me' by Marra PL Lanot from Marra PL. Lanot's *Passion & Compassion* (Mga Tula sa Pilipino at Ingles). Quezon City: New Day Publishers, 1981; 2nd printing, 1988.

Urban Renewal by ko ko thett from Warscape: Urbam Poems from Burma (Sept, 2012).

'Turning The Page' by Mimi Khalvati from In White Ink (Carcanet 1991).

'The Topography of Wellington' by Jennifer Compton from *This City (*Otago University Press 2011).

'Bratislava' by Mary Jo Salter from *The Common* (The Common Foundation).

'On the Cadence of Forgetting' by Ágnes Lehóczky from *Carillonneur* (Shearsman Books, 2014).

Ágnes Lehóczky. All rights reserved. Used by permission of Ágnes Lehóczky.

'Reel' by George Szirtes from Reel (Bloodaxe, 2004). Copyright © 2014 by George Szirtes. All rights reserved. Used by permission of George Szirtes.

'Story of a City' by Moniza Alvi from *Split World* Poems 1990-2005 (Bloodaxe Books 2008) Copyright © 2008 by Moniza Alvi. All rights reserved. Used with the permission of Moniza Alvi and Bloodaxe Books.

'There is no wind in Oslo' by Mark Strand from Smithsonian Magazine (2012), Copyright ©2012 by Mark Strand. Used by permission of Mark Strand.

'My Father's City' by Pascale Petit from *Fauverie (*Seren, *2014).* Copyright © 2014 by Pascale Petit. All rights reserved. Used by permission of Pascale Petit and the publisher Seren)

'Visiting Paris' by Vijay Seshadri. Copyright © by Vijay Seshadri. All rights reserved. Used by permission of Vijay Seshadri.

'Prague' by Khadijah Queen appeared first on the Academy of American Poets site in 2013. Copyright © 2013 by Khadijah Queen. All rights reserved. Used by permission of Khadijah Queen.

'Early Evening, Downtown Tirana' by Morelle Smith from *Tho Way Woods Trav*el (UKA Press, Bristol, UK). Copyrignt © by Morelle Smith. All rights reserved. Used by permission of Morelle Smith.

'Calvaries' by Eugenijus Ališanka from *Dievakaulis. Vilnius: Lietuvos rašytojų sąjungos leidykla* (1999). Copyright © 1999 by Eugenijus Ališanka. All rights reserved. Used by permission of Eugenijus Ališanka.

POETS

Abdoul Mtoka was born and grew up in Bujumbura, Burundi, and earned undergraduate and law degrees at the Université d'Aix-Marseille, France. He won the Michel Kayoya Prize in 2009 for his short story *Le Fils de Buyenzi* (The Son of Buyenzi) and again in 2010 for *Le contraire de l'amour* (The Contradiction of Love). He has also published legal and historical articles.

Abhilash Surendran quit his corporate job to travel the world photographing and writing about the places he visited. He has been to 53 countries so far. He is currently working on a book based on his experiences.

Adam Borzic (born 1978, Prague) is well known Czech poet, essayist, psychotherapist and chief editor of the literary magazine Tvar. He co-founded the poetic group Fantasía. They published a common book *Fantasía* (Dauphin, 2008).He published collection of poems *Rozevírání* (Openning, Dauphin, 2011) and *Pocasí v Evrope* (Weather in Europe, Malvern, 2013), which was nominated for Magnesia Litera 2014, major Czech literary award. His poems were included in the anthology of Best Czech Poems (in 2010, 2012, 2013). He contributes to many print and online journals in Czech Republic. His poems have been translated into English, Croatian and Romanian.

Ágnes Lehóczky is a Hungarian poet and translator born in Budapest. She was one of the translators of the anthology *New Order Hungarian Poets of the Post 1989 Generation*, edited by George Szirtes (Arc, 2010). Her first full collection in English, *Budapest to Babel*, was published by Egg Box Publishing. She was the winner of the Daniil Pashkoff Prize 2010 in poetry, the inaugural winner of the Jane Martin Prize for Poetry at Girton College, Cambridge, in 2011, and received the Bertha Bulcsu-Award (August 2012, Budapest). Lehóczky's second collection in English, *Rememberer*, supported by the Arthur Welton Poetry Award, was also published by Eggbox in 2011.

Ahsan Akbar grew up in Dhaka, Bangladesh. He studied at Exeter, worked as a record seller, bookseller and as an investment banker in the City. He currently runs an arts and media portal in London, and is at work on a novel. Bengal Lights Books published his debut collection of poems, *The Devil's Thumbprint*, in 2013. He is a producer of Hay Festival Dhaka.

Aimé Eyengué is a poet and a Doctor of Social Sciences who graduated in Political Science. A specialist in lifestyles, he is interested in political action and its impact on the fate of nations and people. Initiator of the celebration of 60 years of Congolese literature (1953-2013) and Brazzaville Book Fair since 2013; he is author of several books, including Le conseiller du Prince A Prince de la Paix. He has designed the Fleuvitude as a literary theory.

A.K. Welsapar is the author of more than 20 books. He made his debut as an author with a book for children *Which of us will dive deepest?* (1982) and *The first drop* (1983). His novel *The Melon Head* (1984), was awarded a prize in a Turkmen national literature-competition. *The Pain of Eternal Uncertainties*, Poetry book in Russian, was awarded a prize from Moscow Organisation of the Russian Writers (2012).

Alan Mills, poet and essayist, was born in Guatemala, 1979. His poetry books includes: *Los nombres ocultos*, 2002; *Marca de agua*, 2005; *Poemas sensibles*, 2005; *Testamentofuturo*, 2007; *Síncopes*, 2007; *Syncopes* (french translation), 2010. He has participated in many poetry festivals all over Latin America and Spain, Sweden, Germany and France. Some of his poems have been translated into English, Portuguese, French, German and Italian.

Alex Bramwell was born in 1985 in Sandbach, Cheshire, England. Having graduated from Goldsmiths College, University of London, she has since been working as a librarian organising literary exhibitions and poetry readings. She holds an MA in library and information management. Her poems have appeared in online

publications and in *World Poetry Almanac*; her haikus have been published in *Shamrock Haiku Journal.*

Alfred Corn has published ten books of poems, including *Stake: Selected Poems, 1972-1992* (1999) and, most recently, *Unions* (2014). He has also published a novel, *Part of His Story*, a study of prosody *The Poem's Heartbeat*, and two collections of critical essays, *The Metamorphoses of Metaphor* and *Atlas: Selected Essays, 1989-2007*. For many years he taught in the Graduate Writing Program at Columbia University and held visiting posts at UCLA, the University of Cincinnati, the University of Tulsa, Oklahoma State, and Yale. His book reviews have appeared in the *New York Times Book Review*, the *Nation*, the *New Republic,* the *Hudson Review,* and *Poetry London*.

Ali Al Jallawi is a contemporary Bahraini poet, born in Manama in 1975. He began writing poetry at the age of fourteen. His early work was characterised by revolutionary and political ideas, and he was arrested at the age of seventeen because of a poem. He was arrested again in 1995 and imprisoned until 1998.

Alvin Pang (b. 1972, Singapore) is a poet, writer, editor, anthologist, and translator. His poetry has been translated into over fifteen languages. A Fellow of the University of Iowa's International Writing Program (2002), his publications include *Testing the Silence* (1997), *City of Rain* (2003), *What Gives Us Our Names* (2011). His most recent volumes of poetry, *OTHER THINGS AND OTHER POEMS* (Brutal:Croatia), *Teorija strun* ["String Thoory"] (JKSD:Slovenia) and *WHEN THE BARBARIANS ARRIVE* (Arc Publications,UK), were published in 2012. Pang was named the 2005 Young Artist of the Year for Literature by Singapore's National Arts Council, and was conferred the Singapore Youth Award (Arts and Culture) in 2007.

Amparo Osorio is a major Spanish-language poet who has also written fiction and essays. She is the editor of the literary review Común Presencia; co-founder of the Literary Foundation Común

Presencia and co-founder of the Colombian division of World Poetry Day. She is also co-director of the international literary imprint Los Conjurados. Her poems have been translated into several languages.

Anatoly Kudryavitsky has published three collections, *Shadow of Time* (Goldsmith, 2005), *Morning at Mount Ring* (Doghouse, 2007) and *Capering Moons* (Doghouse, 2011), as well as *A Night in the Nabokov Hotel*, an anthology of contemporary Russian poetry in English translation (Dedalus, 2006), *Bamboo Dreams,* an anthology of Irish haiku (Doghouse, 2012), and three novels. His latest novel, *Disunity,* has been published by Glagoslav Publications (London) in 2013. He lives in Dublin, Ireland, where he edits *Shamrock Haiku Journal*.

Andy Knowlton is an American poet and mixed-media artist currently based in Seoul, South Korea. Knowlton combines street art, music, video, installation art, mass-mail art and various other art forms to give life to his poetry. On the streets of Seoul, Knowlton places hand-made dolls for unsuspecting passers-by to find and keep. The dolls are made out of found trash; each doll holds a bottle containing an original poem by Knowlton.

Annette Hagemann was born in Münster, Germany in 1967. She studied German literature and anthropology at Göttingen University and later worked as a freelance journalist and as a museum educator in the Lower Saxony State Museum Hanover. Since 2001 she worked in the Literature House, Hanover. In 2009, she published her first collection of poetry *Competing with the Sun God*. Also in 2009, she received the literary scholarship of Lower Saxony. Her second poetry collection *Siren of the Shower Room* was published in Berlin in 2014.

Annie Finch, poet, translator, librettist, editor and critic, was born in New Rochelle, New York on October 31, 1956. Finch's books of poetry include *Among the Goddesses: An Epic Libretto in Seven Dreams* (Red Hen Press, 2010);*Calendars* (Tupelo,

2003), shortlisted for the Foreword Poetry Book of the Year Award; *Eve* (Story Line, 1997); and a translation of the *Complete Poems of Louise Labé* (University of Chicago Press, 2006). Her innovative performance poem *The Encyclopedia of Scotland* was published by Salt in 2004.

Anni Sumari (born in Helsinki, Finland,) is a poet and author of 13 books (poems, short prose, a travelogue) published so far. She works as a freelance writer and translates fiction. She has edited several anthologies of Finnish poetry. Sumari was awarded a national book prize titled The Dancing Bear Prize (founded by the Finnish National Broadcasting Co.). She got a 5-year artist grant from the Finnish Ministry of Culture for 2007-2011 and 3-year artist grant 2013-2015. Her poems have been translated and published into 23 languages. She has participated in approx. 70 international literature festivals and worked in several international artists' residencies.

Arthur Sze, born in New York City in 1950, is a second-generation Chinese American. Educated at the University of California, Berkeley, Sze is the author of nine books of poetry, including *Compass Rose* (Copper Canyon Press, 2014); *The Ginkgo Light* (Copper Canyon Press, 2009); *Quipu* (Copper Canyon Press, 2005); *The Redshifting Web: Poems 1970-1998* (Copper Canyon Press, 1998); and *Archipelago* (Copper Canyon Press, 1995). His other collections include *River River* (Lost Roads Publishers, 1987); *Dazzled* (Floating Island Publications, 1982); *Two Ravens* (Tooth of Time Books, 1976; revised, 1984); and *The Willow Wind* (Tooth of Time Books, 1972; revised, 1981). He is also a celebrated translator and released The Silk Dragon: Translations from the Chinese (Copper Canyon Press) in 2001.

Asa Boxer's poetry has garnered several prizes and is included in various anthologies, magazines and literary journals around the world. His books are *The Mechanical Bird* (Signal, 2007), *Skullduggery* (Signal, 2011) and *Friar Biard's Primer to the*

New World (Frog Hollow Press, 2013). Boxer is also founder and manager of the Montreal International Poetry Prize.

Ashjan Al Hendi, born in Jeddah, gained her doctorate in the Department of Language and Arabic Literature at the School of Oriental and African Studies at the University of London. She has published three collections of poetry, *Dream Smell of Rain* (1996), *Rain Has a Taste of Lemon* (2007) and *Riq al-Ghaimat* (2010), as well as a book of literary criticism, *Engagement with Heritage in the Contemporary Poetry of Women in the Arabian Peninsula* (1996). Her poems have been translated into French, German, Spanish and Turkish. She is currently an assistant professor in the Arabic Department of the Faculty of Arts and Humanities in King Abdulaziz University, Jeddah.

Astrid Alben's most recent collection *Ai! Ai! Pianissimo* was published by Arc Publications in 2011. Alben has been described as 'a new and original voice in English poetry, serious and uncompromising' (TLS). Her poems, essays, translations and reviews are widely published in journals, magazines, newspapers and anthologies, and her poetry is translated into several languages. Alben is the editor of three art-science anthologies: *Findings on Ice* (2007), *Findings on Elasticity* (2010) and *Findings on Light* (2015), published by Lars Muller Publications. Alben is a Royal Society of Arts Fellow and Wellcome Trust Fellow.

Beverley Nambozo Nsengiyunva is a Ugandan poet, actress and writer and founder of the Babishai Niwe (BN) Poetry Foundation. Her work has appeared in Drumvoices Revue, Kwani, Postcolonial Journal, Lawino Magazine, Short Story Day Africa, New Black Magazine and many others and has been translated into Luganda, French, Portuguese and Kiswahiili. She is Uganda's 2014 BBC Commonwealth Games Poet for the poem, Lake Nalubaale. She currently lives in Kampala with her husband and children and is working on her first novel – Elgona.

Brigitte Fuchs, born 1951 in Switzerland, writes poetry, short prose, aphorisms and experimental texts. She has received numerous awards, among others Joachim-Ringelnatz-Preis 1991; Meran Poetry Prize 2000; and 2nd Prize at the Rilke Festival Sierre 2003. Her recent publications include: *Salto Wortale*, playful lyrics, edition 8, Zurich 2011 and Es tanzt der Stein, poems, edition 8, Zurich 2014.

Bryan Thao Worra is an award-winning Lao-American writer. He holds an NEA Fellowship in Literature and is the author of 6 books. He is the Creative Works Editor of the Journal on Southeast Asian American Education and Advancement. His work is on display at the Smithsonian's national traveling exhibit 'I Want the Wide American Earth: An Asian Pacific American Story.' His 2013 book *DEMONSTRA* was selected as Book of the Year by the Science Fiction Poetry Association. He served as a Cultural Olympian representing Laos during the 2012 London Summer Games.

Cathal Ó Searcaigh is an Irish poet, playwright and prose writer who writes in the Irish language. He was born in Gortahork, a town in the Gaeltacht region of Donegal, and lives at the foot of Mount Errigal. His collections of poetry include Homecoming/An Bealach 'na Bhaile (1993); Na Buachaillí Bána (1995); Out in the Open (translations by Frank Sewell, 1997); Ag Tnúth leis an tSolas (2001) – for which he received The Irish Times Irish Literature Prize for the Irish language, in 2001; Gúrú i gClúidíní(Guru in Nappies) (2006) and CathalO'Searcaigh's Kathmandu, Poems Selected and New (An English/Nepali Bilingual Edition).

Claire Askew's poetry has been included in numerous publications, including *The Guardian*, *Poetry Scotland, New Writing Scotland* and *PANK*. Her work has also won many accolades, and most recently, Claire has been awarded a Scottish Book Trust New Writers Award (2012), the International Salt Prize for Poetry (2013), and an Edwin Morgan Poetry Award (2014). Her first collection, *This changes things*, was published by Bloodaxe

in February 2016. She holds a PhD in Creative Writing from the University of Edinburgh, and blogs at onenightstanzas.com.

Clive Wilmer was born in Harrogate in 1945, grew up in London, and lives in Cambridge. He is a poet, translator, critic and lecturer, and has published seven volumes of poetry, including his *New and Collected Poems* (Carcanet Press, 2012). He has also published six volumes of poetry translated from Hungarian in collaboration with George Gömöri. He writes for various periodicals, notably *PN Review* and the *Times Literary Supplement*.

Conceição Lima is a Santomean poet from the town of Santana in São Tomé. She studied journalism in Portugal and worked in radio, television and in the print press in her native country. Conceição Lima's poetry has been published in newspapers, magazines, and anthologies in several countries. Her poetry books include O Útero da Casa, A Dolorosa Raiz do Micondó and O País de Akendenguê.

Charlotte Hill O'Neal, aka Mama C, is a vocalist, writer, poet and visual artist who has been performing professionally for more than 20 years and exhibiting her art work extensively since 1986. Mama C was born in Kansas City, Kansas, but left the states at age 19 to live and work in Africa. She has lived in Tanzania since 1972. She is co-director of the united African Alliance Community Center (UAACC) which provides classes in various subjects for the AruMeru Community outside of Arusha, Tanzania.

Chath PierSath was born in Kop Nymit in Banteay Meanchey Province, Cambodia. He is a noted Khmer-American poet and painter. He, his older brother and sister immigrated to the United States in 1981, and lived first in Boulder, Colorado. He graduated from New College of California. His poem, *A Letter to My Mother* appears in *Children of Cambodia's Killing Fields: Memoirs of Survivors* compiled by Dith Pran and edited by Kim DePaul (Yale University Press, 1997). Other works appear in Anthologies of the Merrimack Valley Press of Lowell, Massachusetts. His recent

works include, *After and This Body Mystery*, books of poetry, published by Abingdon Square Publishing.

Chirikure Chirikure was born in 1962 in Gutu, Zimbabwe. He is a Zimbabwean poet, songwriter, and writer. He worked with one of Zimbabwe's leading publishing houses as an editor/publisher for 17 years, until 2002. He now runs a literary agency and also works as a performance poet, cultural consultant and translator. He has written and translated a number of children's stories and published some educational textbooks, and has also been an occasional contributor to the print media and ran a radio programme for young Shona writers.

Christopher Merrill's recent books include *Boat* (poetry), *Necessities* (prose poetry), and *The Tree of the Doves; Ceremony, Expedition, War* (nonfiction). He directs the International Writing Program at the University of Iowa and serves on the U.S. National Commission for UNESCO as well as the National Council on the Humanities. His honors include a Chevalier in the Order of Arts and Letters.

Claudia Patricia Sánchez Carcamo was born in Tegucigalpa, Honduras in 1983. A writer, cultural manager, psychologist, project facilitator, her works have been published in several magazines, newspapers as well as national and international anthologies.

Claus Ankersen (born 1967) is a Danish writer, spoken word-artist and installation artist. He has distinguished himself as an active performing arts author of the literary reading scene. He was particularly co-founder of the literary boyband *Words On Wheels*, curator of the spoken word club 'Wicked Wednesday' and founder of the League Danish Arts Authors and columnist in the morning newspaper Date.

Colin Channer is a Jamaican writer, often referred to as *Bob Marley* with a pen, due to the spiritual, sensual, social themes presented from a literary Jamaican perspective. Indeed, his first

two full-length novels, *Waiting in Vain* and *Satisfy My Soul,* bear the titles of well-known Marley songs. He has also written the short story collection *Passing Through,* and the novellas *I'm Still Waiting* and *The Girl with the Golden Shoes*. Some of his short stories have been anthologized.

Delroy 'Nesta' Williams is a poet/short story writer from Dominica. He has participated in and organized many poetry showcases and activities and is currently a committee member of the Nature Island Literary Festival. He self-published his first book of poetry – *One Room Shack*. The book received positive reviews and Nesta has already put the finishing touches on his second and third books *Moods and Attitudes* and *Shades of the Same.* He won Dominica's Independence Celebrations literary award for short story in 2012 and 2013.

Denize Lauture was born in Haiti, the first of thirteen children, and migrated from Haiti to the United States in 1968. His poetry has been published in many countries, including the West Indies, Spain, and Canada. In the United States, his poetry has appeared in various literary magazines, including *Callaloo*, *Black American Literature Forum*, and *African Commentary*. *Father and Son* was one of five books nominated to receive the National Association for the Advancement of Colored People's (NAACP) 1993 Image Award. Lauture teaches at Saint Thomas Aquinas College in Sparkill, New York, where he was the recipient of the 1994 Board of Trustees' Award for Excellence.

Derek Walcott, poet and playwright, born on the island of Saint Lucia, a former British colony in the West Indies, was trained as a painter but turned to writing as a young man. He published his first poem in the local newspaper at the age of 14. Five years later, he borrowed $200 to print his first collection, *25 Poems*. Walcott's major breakthrough came with the collection *In a Green Night: Poems 1948-1960* (1962). His recent collections include *Tiepolo's Hound* (2000), *The Prodigal* (2004), *Selected Poems* (edited by

Edward Baugh, 2007) and White Egrets (2010). In 1992, Walcott won the Nobel Prize in Literature.

Dhabiya Khamis is an author, translator and diplomat with over 45 published works, including 18 poetry collections, 4 works of fiction, 9 volumes of essays and 12 translated works. Born in August 1958, she has an MA in Arabic Literature from American University in Cairo and a BA in Politial Science from Indiana University, Bloomington, USA. She was a diplomat with the Arab League (1992-2009), and served as UAE Ambassador to India (2004-2005).

Dunya Mikhail was born in Baghdad, Iraq in 1965 and left to the US in mid 1990s for the sake of poetry and freedom of writing. She has six books in Arabic, three in English, and one in Italian. They include *The Iraqi Nights*, *Diary of A Wave Outside the Sea*, and *The War Works Hard,* in addition to editing a pamphlet of *15 Iraqi Poets.* Her honors include Kresge fellowship (2013), Arab American Book Award (2010), Griffin shortlist (2006), and UN Human Rights award (2001). She works as a lecturer of Arabic at Oakland University in Michigan.

Edwin Madrid was born in Quito in 1961. He has served as a cultural journalist for various national and foreign newspapers. Their texts have appeared in magazines and newspapers as well as in major anthologies of Ecuador and Latin America. He has received awards: National Youth Poetry Award *Djenana Guayaquil*, 1989; Ecuadorian National Writers Award 90, Quito, 1991. In 1992 he was semifinalist Casa de las Américas Prize in Cuba with his book: Horses and iguanas Poetry Prize 2004 Casa de America, Madrid-Spain.

Elizabeth Orlando was born and raised on Long Island, New York. She graduated with honors from Mount Vernon College and the University of Akron, School of Law in Akron in Ohio. She joined the Foreign Service of the U.S. Department of State as

a diplomatic courier. Through her almost twelve years of travel, Betsy has written impressionistic poems and short stories about and in the places she has lived and visited.

Ernesto Cardenal Martínez is a Nicaraguan Catholic priest, poet and politician. He is a liberation theologian and the founder of the primitivist art community in the Solentiname Islands, where he lived for more than ten years (1965–1977). Born in Granada, Nicaragua in 1925, Cardenal studied literature first in Managua, Mexico. Later, New York and traveled through Italy, Spain and Switzerland between 1949 and 1950. The most comprehensive collection of his poetry in English translation is *Pluriverse: New and Selected Poems* (New Directions, 2009).

Ester Fenoll García (b.1967) is known for her use of different languages in her poetry. She has published two collections, *Esmorzar perfecte* (2006) and *Anticipant Octubre* (2008), and has won several literary awards, including the Premi Grandalla de Poesía in 2005. Teresa Colom, a major voice in Catalan literature, has praised the freshness of Ester Fenoll's poetry.

Eugenijus Ališanka (b. 1960 in Barnaul, Russia) is a poet, essayist and translator. Since 2003, he has been working as a chief editor of magazine Vilnius, published in English (The Vilnius Review) and Russian languages. He has published five books of poetry and two essay collections. In 1992, *Equinox* (1991) won the Zigmas Gėlė Award. *The Return of Dionysus* (2001) has received the Lithuanian Culture Ministry Award. Ališanka has translated poetry by Wisława Szymborska, Carolyn Forché, Dannie Abse, among others. Ališanka has also received a 'Spring of Poetry' award for translation of poetry.

Françoise Roy was born in Quebec City, Canada in 1959. She lives in Mexico since 1992. She has won National Translation Award in Poetry; Jacqueline Déry-Mochon Novel Award; Alonso Vidal National Poetry Award; Ditet e Naimit International Poetry Award (Macedonia); International Grand Prize for Poetry of the Orient-Occident Academy (Romania). She has published novels, short

stories and thirteen poetry collections and has been granted artistic residences and grants in Mexico, Argentina and Canada. She has participated in poetry fests worldwide and translated some sixty books.

Frank Mkalawile Chipasula, poet and editor, earned a BA at the University of Zambia, an MA in African American Studies at Yale University, and both an MA in creative writing and a PhD in English literature at Brown University. Exiled from his native Malawi, Chipasula frequently engages themes of censorship and exile. His poetry collections include *Visions and Reflections* (1972), *O Earth, Wait for Me* (1984), and *Whispers in the Wings: New and Selected Poems* (2001). Chipasula's honors include the BBC Poetry Prize and two Pushcart Prize nominations.

Gabeba Baderoon is a South African poet and the author of three collections of poetry - *The Dream in the Next Body* (Kwela/Snailpress, 2005), *The Museum of Ordinary Life* (DaimlerChrysler, 2005) and *A hundred silences*(Kwela/Snailpress, 2006). Her poetry is included in the anthologies, *Worldscapes*, *Ten Hallam Poets*, *Voices from All Over* and Birds in Words, and in journals. Gabeba is the recipient of the *DaimlerChrysler Award for South African Poetry 2005* and held the *Guest Writer Fellowship* at the Nordic Africa Institute in Sweden in 2005.

Gabriel Rosenstock (born 1949) is an Irish writer who works chiefly in the Irish language. A member of Aosdána, he is a poet, haikuist and translator. He has written or translated over one hundred books. Two of his more recent works are Eachtraí Krishnamurphy (2003) and Krishnamurphy Ambaist (2004). He appears in the anthology Best European Fiction 2012, edited by Aleksandar Hemon, with a preface by Nicole Krauss (Dalkey Archive Press).

George Szirtes was born in Hungary in 1948 and came to England as a refugee in 1956. Having studied Fine Art, he published his first book of poems, T*he Slant Door* in 1979. It won the Faber

Memorial Prize. He has published many since then, winning the T S Eliot Prize for *Reel* in 2004, and was shortlisted for the same prize for his two subsequent books *The Burning of the Books* (2009) and *Bad Machine* (2013). His *New and Collected Poems* appeared in 2008. He is also a prize-winning translator of poetry and fiction from Hungarian into English.

Gerard Noiret is a French poet and novelist born in 1948. He has worked in various magazines - including literary fortnightly newspapers and magazines. Some of his texts were brought to the scene or put voice to the Radio1. He also works as a trainer and writing workshop facilitator. Author of poetry and novels, he is a member of the board of the journal Europe.

Germain Droogenbroodt is a poet, translator, publisher and promoter of modern international poetry. So far he has written eight poetry books and translated more than thirty collections of German, Italian, Spanish, English and French poetry, including anthologies of Bertolt Brecht, Reiner Kunze, Peter Huchel, Miguel Hernández, José Ángel Valente, Francisco Brines and Juan Gil-Albert and rendered Arabic, Chinese, Japanese, Persian and Korean poetry into Dutch. As founder and editor of POINT Editions (POetry INTernational) he has published more than eighty collections of mainly modern, international poetry, including an anthology of modern poets from Taiwan, published in Dutch, English and German.

G. Mend-Ooyo was born in Dar'ganga, Mongolia. After having taught for several years, he became reporter and literary editor of the Mongolian radio and in 1981 general editor of the National Mongolian Television. He is the president of the Mongolian PEN-Club and founded the Mongolian Academy of Culture, and GUNU, a magazine for culture, literature and poetry. His oeuvre contains over 20 books of poetry, narrative and essays. He is president and organizer of the XXVII World Congress of Poets, Mongolia.

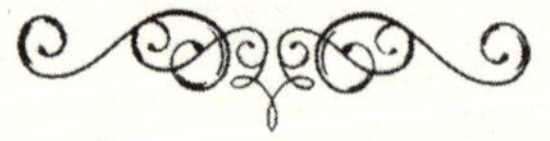

Grandmaster Masese is a young musician based in Nairobi, Kenya, fusing traditional instrumental music, poetry and spoken word. He plays Obukano, an ancient instrument from the Gusii(aka Kisii) community from western Kenya, Nyanza province.

Gwen Burnyeat is a Leverhulme Trust Scholar, student fellow of the Royal Anthropological Institute, and member of civil society network Rodeemos el Diálogo. She has published academic articles on transitional justice and communities in Colombia, short fiction in the *Dublin Review*, and a recent essay on Gabriel García Márquez in a collection called *Was Gabo an Irishman?* She lived in Asunción for six months teaching English on her gap year in 2004-5.

Hamid Ismailov born in an ancient city, in what is now Kyrgyzstan, is an Uzbek novelist and poet. He was forced to leave his home in Tashkent when his writing brought him to the attention of government officials. Under threat of arrest, he moved to London and joined the BBC World Service, where he is now Head of the Central Asian Service. Ismailov is a prolific writer of poetry and prose, and his books have been published in Uzbek, Russian, French, German, Turkish, English and other languages. He is the author of many novels including *Sobranie Utonchyonnyh*, *Le Vagabond Flamboyant* among others; and poetry collections including *Sad* (Garden) and *Pustynya* (Desert).

Hasso Krull, poet and essayist, was born in 1964. He studied Estonian language and literature at Tallinn's University of Pedagogy. He has published several collections of poetry, written numerous essays and literary reviews. Krull's poems have been translated into Finnish, Swedish, English, French and Latvian. In 2004 the epic *Meeter ja Demeeter* (Metre and Demeter) appeared, based on folklore of many different nations and won the Baltic Assembly Prize for Literature in 2005. His poetry collection *Neli korda neli* (Four Times Four, 2009) was granted the poetry award of the Cultural Endowment of Estonia.

Hatto Fischer, who lives in Athens, is a writer, poet, educator, philosopher, political scientist and a humanist with studies at the Carleton University in Ottawa, Canada, the London School of Economics, and further studies on philosophy at the Philosophical Seminar in Heidelberg. He is also a coordinator of the Non-Profit Urban Society POIEIN KAI PRATTEIN—*'to create is to do.'*

Ibrahim Waheed 'Ogaru' is a professional educator and statesman turned writer, artist, musician and television personality, multi-faceted Maldivian celebrity, the recipient of the Sahitya Akademi (India) Munshi Premchand Fellowship Award in 2008, and the SAARC Literary Award in 2011. His articles, stories and poetry in Dhivehi and English have been published in the Maldives, India, Pakistan, Sri Lanka, Bangladesh, the U.K and the U.S.A.

Ilona Yusuf spent her early childhood in England, where she was born. Later, her family moved to Lahore, Pakistan, where she was educated. She is a published poet and the editor for the Alhamra Literary Review, a collection of writings by Pakistani and South Asian writers in English. *Picture This...* is her first book of poems. She also designs lamps and furniture, both of which she likes to call 'conversation pieces' as they often incorporate the use of her photographs. She divides her time between Islamabad, Pakistan and Scottsdale, Arizona.

Immanuel Mifsud was born in Malta in 1967. He started writing poetry and prose when he was 16, and also began working with experimental theatre groups, directing his own plays and later works by Chekhov, Dario Fo, Max Frisch, Federico Garcia Lorca, David Mamet, Harold Pinter and Alfred Buttigieg. Various works by Immanuel Mifsud have been translated and published in a number of European countries and USA. Mifsud's prose immediately caught the attention of Maltese critics and won him the tag as the Maltese Generation-X writer.

Inara Cedrins was a poet and a translator. Her anthology of contemporary Latvian poetry was published by the University of

Iowa Press, and her new Baltic anthology, three books of poetry from Latvia, Lithuania and Estonia, was published by the University of New Orleans Press, with her prints as cover art.

Indah Widiastuti (born 1971) is a faculty in Department of Architecture, SAPPK – Institut Teknologi Bandung (ITB), Indonesia. She completed her Undergraduate and Post Graduate education in Architecture in Institut Teknologi Bandung (ITB), and her PhD in Anna University Chennai. She started writing poems in 2010 during her 4 years stays in India. Her poems have been published in various popular e-magazines, mostly in India, such as the Stagebuzz (May Issue 2011, India), Indian Ruminations (May Issue 2011, India), and Indian Ruminations (May Issue 2011, India), Brown Critique (December 2012 issue, India), and Gulmohar Magazine (April 2014).

Indran Amirthanayagam is a Sri Lankan-American poet-diplomat, essayist and translator in English, Spanish and French. Indran Amirthanayagam's *The Elephants Of Reckoning* won the 1994 Paterson Poetry Prize. He writes poetry and essays in English, Spanish and French. His Spanish collections include *El Infierno de los Pajaros* and *El Hombre que Recoge Nidos*. He has also published *Ceylon R.I.P.*

Irina Grivnina was born in Fergana, Uzbekistan, in 1945. A dissident writer, literary critic and translator, she lived in Moscow and was a member of the Moscow Helsinki Group. In 1980 she was arrested by the KGB, and imprisoned for 14 months. In 1985, she immigrated to the Netherlands. She has since been living in Amsterdam working as a literary translator and a free-lance journalist. She writes for newspapers, magazines and the BBC Russian Service. Her novel titled *General's Daughter* was published in Moscow in 2005.

Ishaq Imruh Bakari was born in Basseterre, capital of St. Kitts & Nevis. He represented St. Kitts & Nevis at Poetry Parnassus, the international Poetry Festival staged at London's Southbank

Centre as part of the *Cultural Olympiad* organized for the 2012 Olympics. His published works include *Sounds & Echoes* (Karnak House, 1980), *Secret Lives* (Bogle L'Ouverture, 1986). He lectures in Film Studies at the University of Winchester, and lives between the UK and East Africa.

Jael Uribe is the pen name of Elizabeth Medina, a Dominican writer, storyteller, poet and painter creator of the female poetic foundation named Women Poets International. Born in 1975, she is considered the initiator of the *Women Scream* International Poetry Festival, an event celebrated worldwide to honor women against violence.

James V. Dwalu was born in Bandor Town, Grand Cape Mount County, Liberia. He has been writing since 1985. He has self-published two books, *Off to School We Go* (2004) and *Fun in the Interior* (2009). WE-CARE published two of his books in 2009: *Varney and The Monkey Bridge* and *Blama's Dream*. He mainly writes poems and stories for children. He is a member of the Liberia Association of Writers.

Jan Napier is Western Australian poet and short story writer whose work won the 2014 Creatix prize for poetry. Her writings have been published in journals and anthologies within Australia and beyond including in *Famous Reporter, Poetry New Zealand, dotdotdash, Unusual Work, Speed Poets, The Mozzie*, and other journals. She was the in house reviewer of Antipodean SF between 2009 and 2012. *In 2011, Jan broke both of her wrists, resulting in permanent disability.*

Jean Portante was born in 1950 in Differdange (Luxembourg), of Italian parents. He lives in Paris. His work, rich with forty books – poetry, novels, essays, plays, is widely translated. In France, he is a member of the Académie Mallarmé. He is recipient of many awards.

Jekwu Ozoemene is a banker, poet and playwright. He is the author of *Shadows of Existence: An Anthology of Poetry* (2009). One of his Poems appeared in the recently released *Poems for a century: An anthology on Nigeria* edited by Tope Omoniyi.

Jelena Lengold (b.1959) is a storyteller, novelist and a poet. She has published five books of poetry, one novel (Baltimore, 2003, 2011) and four books of stories, including *Pokisli lavovi* (Rain-soaked Lions, 1994), Lift (Lift, 1999) and *Vašarski mađioničar* (The Fairground Magician, 2008, 2009). She has been represented in several anthologies of poetry and stories, and her works have been translated into several languages. Lengold worked as a journalist and an editor for ten years in the cultural department of Radio Belgrade. She worked as a project coordinator in the Conflict Management programme of Nansenskolen Humanistic Academy in Lillehammer, Norway.

Jennifer Compton was born in New Zealand but immigrated to Australia in the early 70s. She is a poet and a playwright. Her first book of poetry *From the Other Woman* was published as part of the Five Islands New Poet Series in 1993. *Aroha* was published by Flarestack Press in the UK in 1998. Then there was *Blue – Indigo Imprint* at Ginninderra Press – in 2000 which was shortlisted for the NSW Premier's Prize in 2001. *Barefoot,* published by Picaro Press in 2010 was shortlisted for the John Bray Poetry Award at the Adelaide Festival in 2012. *This City*, published by Otago University Press in July 2011 won the Kathleen Grattan Award in New Zealand.

Joris Lenstra is a translator and writer. He has a Master's degree in literature. He has translated *Jack Kerouac*, *Walt Whitman*, and *Lawrence Ferlinghetii*, and *Oscar Wilde* into Dutch. He loves to write poetry, short stories and articles. He believes that the ability to write makes him a better translator; he always looks for the flow in the texts that he produces and is not satisfied with mere literal translation.

Jumoke Verissimo was born in Lagos, Nigeria. She has worked as a journalist, copywriter, sub-editor and editor. Her award-winning collection of poems, *I am Memory* explores and experiments with the idea of memory on personal and societal levels. She has been a guest poet at the 48th Struga Poetry Evenings, Macedonia and 15th Norwegian Literature Festival in Lillehammer, Norway. Some of her poems have been translated into Arabic, Turkish, Mongolian, Macedonian, Japanese, and Norwegian.

Kapka Kassabova is the author of the travel books *Street Without a Name* (2008), about communist and post-communist Bulgaria, and *Twelve Minutes of Love* (2011), a story of Argentine tango and the search for home. Her poetry collections are *Someone else's life* and *Geography for the Lost*. Born and raised in Sofia, she was educated in New Zealand and now lives in the Scottish Highlands. She is a regular contributor to The Guardian, Intelligent Life, and The Scottish Review of Books.

Karla Brundage is a poet, performance artist, essayist, mother and teacher. She writes mainly of the topics of single motherhood, the complexities of black love relationships and co-parenting in the hip-hop era, mixed race identity and politics. She currently lives and writes in Abidjan, Cote d'Ivoire, where she teaches English. She has also lived or, worked in Honolulu, Hawaii, Zimbabwe, Ghana, Tanzania, New York and Oakland, California, which (along with Ka'a'awa) she considers home. Karla Brundage has one collection of poetry *Swallowing Watermelons*, published by Ishmael Reed Publications.

Karl Schembri (b. 1978) is a Maltese poet, short story writer and editor of the independent weekly newspaper Malta Today. He is a sociology graduate from the University of Malta and has written a collection of short stories, Taħt il-Kappa tax-Xemx (Malta: Minima, 2002) and a novel, Il-Manifest tal-Killer (Malta: Choppy, 2006). He published his first poems with three other poets in the anthology Frekwenzi ta' Spirti fis-Sakra (Malta: 1997).

Katerina Iliopoulou is a poet and translator who lives and works in Athens, Greece. She has published five books of poetry, the most recent is *Every place, once, and completely,* 2015. She has translated the work of Sylvia Plath (*Ariel*), and also Mina Loy, Ted Hughes, Robert Hass and Walt Whitman into Greek. She has been invited to present her work in a number of international poetry festivals and her poetry has been translated and published in many languages. She is co-editor of greekpoetrynow.com and editor in chief of [FRMK], a biannual journal on poetry, poetics and visual arts.

Khadijah Queen is the author of Conduit (Black Goat/Akashic Books 2008) and Black Peculiar (2011), which won the Noemi Press book award for poetry and was a finalist for the Gatewood Prize at Switchback Books. Individual poems and prose have appeared in Jubilat, Aufgabe, Best American Nonrequired Reading (Houghton Mifflin 2010), Rattle, The Volta Book of Poets, Tupelo Quarterly, Eleven Eleven, Memoir, Everyman's Pocket Library of Villanelles (Random House 2012), Fire and Ink: A Social Action Anthology (University of Arizona 2009) and The Force of What's Possible (Nightboat 2014). She has performed her work nationally and internationally, and since 2008 has curated the multi-genre reading series Courting Risk.

Kim Gyeongmee began her literary career by winning the first prize for poetry from Joong Ang Daily Newspaper. She has published three books of poems: Can't I Continue Writing the Suspended Letter Again (1989), For the Selfish Sorrows (1995), and Shh, My concubine is (2001), as well as two books of photo essays, The Sea Comes to Me (2004), and The Lastborn (2006). She won the Nojak Literary Award in 2005 and the Best Radio Writer Award from the Korean TV & Radio Writers Association in 2007. Currently, she is working for KBS as a writer while pursuing a master's degree in Korean literature at Korea University.

Kim Roberts is the author of four books of poems, most recently *To the South Pole*, a series of blank verse sonnets based on the

journals of Antarctic explorer Robert Falcon Scott. She is editor of the literary journal *Beltway Poetry Quarterly* and the anthology *Full Moon on K Street: Poems About Washington, DC*, and co-edits the web exhibit *DC Writers' Homes*.

Ko Ko Thett, poet, translator and editor was born in Rangoon (Yangon) in 1972. He lives in Belgium and is the Burmese editor for the Poetry International website and co-editor and translator of *Bones Will Crow*: 15 Contemporary Burmese Poets, an anthology of Burmese poetry, recipient of the 2012 English PEN Writers in Translation Programme Award and one of '10 books that chart the country's tumultuous history', according to the Guardian. His book of poems, The Burden of Being Burmese, is forthcoming from Zephyr Press, the first ever full-length collection in English by a Burmese poet.

Kwame Dawes is the author of nineteen books of poetry and numerous other books of fiction, criticism, and essays. He has edited over a dozen anthologies. His latest collection, *Duppy Conqueror: New and Selected Poems* (Copper Canyon) appeared in 2013. He is Glenna Luschei Editor of Prairie Schooner and teaches at the University of Nebraska and the Pacific MFA Program. He is Director of the African Poetry Book Fund and Artistic Director of the Calabash International Literary Festival.

Ladan Osman was born in Somalia. She earned a BA at Otterbein College and an MFA at the University of Texas at Austin's Michener Center for Writers. Her poetry has been featured in former US Poet Laureate Ted Kooser's syndicated newspaper column, *American Life in Poetry*. Her poetry is centered on her Somali and Muslim heritage, and has been published in a number of prominent literary magazines. **In 2014 her poetry collection** *The Kitchen Dweller's Testimomy* won the annual Sillerman First Book Prize for African Poets. Osman lives in Chicago.

Lauren K. Alleyne is the author of Difficult Fruit (Peepal Tree Press, 2014). She is originally from Trinidad and Tobago. She

holds a Master of Fine Arts degree from Cornell University, and an MA in English and Creative Writing from Iowa State University. Alleyne's fiction, non-fiction, interviews and poetry have been widely published in journals and anthologies such as Guernica, The Caribbean Writer, Black Arts Quarterly, The Cimarron Review, Crab Orchard Review and Gathering Ground among others. She is currently the Poet-in-Residence, and an Assistant Professor of English at the University of Dubuque.

Lelawattee Manoo-Rahming is a Trinidadian Bahamian poet, fiction writer, and artist. Lelawattee has won the *David Hough Literary Prize* (2001) and the *Canute A. Brodhurst Prize* (2009) from The Caribbean Writer. She has also won the Commonwealth Broadcasting Association 2001 Short Story Competition. Her first book of poetry, *Curry Flavour*, was published in 2000 by Peepal Tree Press. Her second collection of poetry, *Immortelle and Bhandaaraa Poems*, was shortlisted for the Inaugural *Proverse Literary Prize* (2009) was published in 2011 by Proverse Hong Kong.

Les Wicks is an Australian poet who is known for his versatility on both stage and page. He has toured widely and seen publication in over 300 different magazines, anthologies and newspapers across 19 countries in 10 languages. His 11th book of poetry is *Sea of Heartbreak (Unexpected Resilience)* from Puncher & Wattmann, Australia's leading poetry imprint.

Linda M. Deane is a British-born Barbadian poet, essayist and storyteller. She is co-founder of ArtsEtc, a publishing company in Barbados and co-editor, with Robert Edison Sandiford, of *Shouts from the Outfield: The Arts Etc Cricket Anthology* (2007). She is a recipient of a Frank Collymore Literary Endowment and Prime Minister's Award for the poetry collection *Cutting Road Blues* (in press). Her work appears in *Bim, The Understanding Between Foxes and Light* (2013); and most recently in *Give the Ball to the Poet*, A New Anthology of Caribbean Poetry (2014).

Liyou Libsekal is an Ethiopian poet living in Addis Ababa, Ethiopia. She grew up traveling and living mainly in East Africa. Liyou's chapbook, *Bearing Heavy Things* will be part of the African Poetry Book Fund's New Generation African Poets series in 2015.

Lola Koundakjian is an Armenian poet who has lived in New York City since 1979. Her poetry has appeared online in alpialdelapalabra (Argentina), Armenian Poetry Project (New York City), The Literary Groong (University of Southern California), Crime Poetry Weekly, Poetas Siglo XXI, Mediterranean nu (Sweden) and, UniVerse (Chicago); and in print in the Anthology Memoria del XX Festival Internacional de Poesía de Medellin (Colombia), Fórnix 12 (Lima, Peru) Mizna (Vol 13, 2, USA), Kragan Spiurk – Literary Diaspora (Armenia), Armenian Weekly (Boston, USA) and Pakin (Beirut, Lebanon). Lola's work was translated into Arabic, Asturian, French, Spanish and Ukrainian.

Luca Benassi was born in 1976 in Rome. His published collections of poems are: *In the Sidelines of History* (2000), *The Glories of the Grey* (2005), *The Honour of Dust* (2009), *I Will Be Told* (2011) and *The Snow Ford* (2012). He translated into Italian the work of Dutch poet Germain Droogenbroodt *De Weg* [Il Cammino-The Path, 2002]. He published a book of essays on Italian contemporary poetry *Throttled Streams - Italian poets in the third millennium* in 2010. Together with Salvatore Ritrovato and Manuel Cohen, he is the editor of the poetry series *Percorsi* of Puntoacapo Publishing and of the *Almanac of Italian poetry*.

Lucija Stupica was born in 1971 in Celje, Slovenia. She is a poet and an interior designer. Her first book of poetry *Čelo na soncu* [Forehead in the Sun], published in 2000, won the award of the 17th Slovenian Book Fair for the best first book as well as the Zlata ptica (Golden Bird) award for the best artistic achievements. In 2010 she was awarded the German Hubert Burda Prize for young Eastern European poets. Her poetry has been translated into more than fifteen languages worldwide.

Lucy Cristina Chau was born in Panamá in 1971. She has received several awards, among them: Premio Centroamericano de Literatura Rogelio Sinán 2010, Ricardo Miró Poetry Prize 2008 and the Gustavo Batista Cedeño National Poetry Prize for Young poets, in 2006. She is currently professor of Creative Writing in the English teaching program at the Universidad de las Américas, Panamá. Among her publications are: *La Casa Rota*; *IndiGentes*; *La Virgen de la Cueva*, and the story book *De la puerta hacia adentro.* She has represented her country in numerous literary events in America and has collaborated with several literary publications.

Luis Bravo is a poet, performer, essayist, literature Professor. He has born in 1957 and has published ten volumes of poetry since 1984, in books and in multimedia format. Significant among these are: ÁrbolVeloz, an avant-garde work in latinoamerican multimedia poetry (1998); Tamudando (2010) performed and recorded live at the Zavala Muniz Theatre in Montevideo. Bravo's poems have been published in magazines and anthologies in Latin America and Europe and have been translated to English, French, Germany, Swedish, Estonian, Portuguese and Farsi.

Luis Chaves was born in Costa Rica in 1969. He is a poet and narrator and has been published in Costa Rica, Argentina, Mexico, Spain and Germany. Poetry National Prize 2012 (awarded by the Ministry of Culture). He has been elected resident for the Artists in Berlin Program 2015.

Magdalena Horvat (b. 1978 in Skopje, Macedonia) is the author of two poetry collections in Macedonian. Her poems have also been published in English and Catalan in the anthology *Europa* és *una dona. Europe is a Woman* (Universitat Autonoma de Barcelona, 2007).

Mahmoud Darwish is considered to be the most important Arab poet today. He was the editor of Ittihad Newspaper before leaving in 1971 to study for a year in the USSR. Then he went to

Egypt where he worked in Cairo for Al-Ahram Newspaper and in Beirut, Lebanon as an editor of the Journal *Palestinian Issues*. His poems are known throughout the Arab world, and several of them have been put to music. He has published around 30 poetry and prose collections, which have been translated into 35 languages.

Marcela Sulak is the author of a chapbook and two collections of poems, *Immigrant,* and the forthcoming *Decency*, both with Black Lawrence Press. She's translated three poetry collections from the Democratic Republic of the Congo, and from the Czech Republic. For years she worked as a free-lance writer for a Sephardic Foundation in Venezuela, an English teacher in Germany, and a Spanish and English teacher in Ceske Budejovice.

Marcelo Ensema Nsang was born in 1947 in Equatorial Guinea, the only Spanish-speaking country in Africa. Marcelo left Guinea in 1961 to study at the seminary in Granada (Spain) and was ordained a priest in 1973. During his stay in Granada, Marcelo began writing poetry when he became involved with a literary movement called *Redondela.*

Marcos Freitas lives in Brasília since 2001. He is an engineer, poet and professor. He is the author of the books *Life feels itself, The third bank without a river, At a river bend, Mungubas,* and *Unquietness of hours and flowers* among others.

Mark McWatt is a Guyanese poet and fiction writer. He has published three collections of poetry, *Interiors* (1989), *The Language of El Dorado* (1994) that was awarded the Guyana Prize for Poetry, and his latest book of poetry, *The Journey to Le Repentir* (2009). *Suspended Sentences: Fictions of Atonement* (2005), his collection of short stories, won several literary prizes including the Commonwealth Writers' Prize, the Guyana Prize for Literature, and the Casa de las Americas Prize. He has also written numerous academic articles on Caribbean Literature, and is the joint editor of *The Oxford Book of Caribbean Verse* (2005).

Mariama Khan was born in Gambia. Her first collection of poems, Futa Toro, was published in 2003. In 2004, she co-published another volume, *Juffureh: kissing you with hurting lips*, with Bamba Khan, her brother. They also co-authored *Proverbs of the Senegambia*. She also works as an African film producer and director. One of her films, Sutura, won a prize in the 2008 United Nations Population Fund Agency's (UNFPA) Pan-African Film Festival.

Marina Khlebnikova was born and lived in Odessa, Ukraine. Having graduated from Odessa Polytechnical Institute, she worked as an engineer and as a computer programmer. In 1992 she graduated from Moscow Literary Institute in Russia; her poems appeared in Russian and Ukrainian literary magazines. She committed suicide in 1998, just before the publication of her first collection, *Hearing Test*, which has since been published as an e-book and garnered critical acclaim.

Mark Strand born in Canada was the author of numerous collections of poetry, including *Collected Poems* (Alfred A. Knopf, 2014); *Almost Invisible* (Alfred A. Knopf, 2012); *New Selected Poems* (Alfred A. Knopf, 2007); *Man and Camel* (Alfred A. Knopf, 2006); *Blizzard of One* (Alfred A. Knopf, 1998), which won the Pulitzer Prize.

Marra PL. Lanot is a Filipina poet, essayist, and journalist. She is a resident fellow of the University of the Philippines Institute of Creative Writing, where she also teaches at the College of Arts and Letters. Her works – poems, essays, profiles, and teleplays – have won her acclaim in terms of the Palanca Awards, Talaang Ginto, and Catholic Mass Media Awards. In 1998, she became the literary editor of the magazine Mirror Weekly.

Mary Jo Salter is the author of seven books of poetry, most recently *Nothing by Design.* A frequent reviewer and essayist, she is also a lyricist whose song cycle *Rooms of Light*, with

music by Fred Hersch, premiered at Lincoln Center in 2007. Her children's book *The Moon Comes Home* appeared in 1989; her play *Falling Bodies* premiered in 2004. She is also co-editor, with Margaret Ferguson and Jon Stallworthy, of *The Norton Anthology of Poetry* (4th edition, 1996; 5th edition, 2005). Salter became a permanent member of the Writing Seminars faculty in 2007, after 23 years of teaching at Mount Holyoke College. She is presently serving as co-chair of the department.

Mathias Ospelt was born in 1963. He is an author, cabaret artist, organizer and director of studies (at the Adult Education Stein Egerta). Since 1995 he has written 15 cabaret programmes, four plays, three festivals and three musical librettos. He also brought out six books (including regional studies), translated children's books, wrote countless columns and glosses and worked as a songwriter for Liechtenstein bands and music projects. For his literary work he has received several awards.

Mathura (aka Margus Lattik) is an Estonian writer, artist and critic. He has published eight volumes of poetry and a travelogue, in addition to numerous other translations, essays and articles. He is the author of eight collections of poetry and translator of various writers from Mirabai to Kunwar Narain, as well as Dylan Thomas, Ben Okri et al. He is a recipient of several scholarships and has repeatedly been nominated to various Estonian literary awards.

Matthew Shenoda earned his BA from Oregon State University and MFA from the University of Arizona. Shenoda's first book, *Somewhere Else* (2005), won an American Book Award and the inaugural Hala Maksoud Award for Emerging Voice and was named one of the year's top debut books by *Poets & Writers* magazine. His second book is *Seasons of Lotus, Seasons of Bone* (2009). Shenoda is also the editor of Kwame Dawes's *Duppy Conquerer: New and Selected Poems* (2013). He is on the editorial board of the African Poetry Book Series and lives in Chicago with his family.

Mehvash Amin's poems have been part of an anthology, 'Tangerine in the Sun'. They have been published in Vallum, New International POETICS (Canada) The Missing Slate (Pakistan), Sugar Mule (US), and the Atlantic Review (US). Her poem, 'Karachi' published in The Missing Slate, was nominated for the Pushcart Prize, 2013. It was also runner-up in World Cup poetry competition held online by The Missing Slate. She is the editor of anthology of Pakistani poetry and prose, The Aleph Review.

Meg Pierce is an international school teacher currently teaching English in Cote d'Ivoire. She student-taught in Trinidad and Tobago, then volunteered in the Peace Corps in Macedonia. Returning to the U.S., she earned an additional teaching credential in history while teaching in a variety of settings.

Michael Glover was educated at Firth Park Grammar School and read English at Queens' College, Cambridge. Glover has contributed regularly to The Independent, The Times, The Financial Times, The New Statesman and The Economist. He is also a London correspondent for ArtNews, New York, and editor of on-line international poetry forum The Bow-Wow Shop. His seventh collection of poetry, *Only So Much*, was launched in September 2011 by the Sheffield-based Savage Poets Collective.

Michelle Cahill is a Sydney-based writer who was born in Kenya and lived in London before migrating to Australia. She wrote *The Accidental Cage* (IP) which was shortlisted in the Judith Wright Prize and nominated for the *Sydney Morning Herald*'s Best Books. Her second collection *Vishvarūpa* (5 IP) was shortlisted in the Victorian Premier's Literary Awards and the Alec Bolton Prize. She edited *Poetry Without Borders*, co-edited *Contemporary Asian Australian Poets* (Puncher and Wattmann) in 2013 and is founding editor of *Mascara Literary Review.*

Milan Dobričić (b.1977, Belgrade) is a poet, prose writer, translator and editor. He is one of the founders of the cultural NGO Treći Trg (Third Square) which publishes the electronic and printed

literary and art magazine *Treći Trg* (www.trecitrg.org.rs), where he works as editor. His poetry and prose has been published in various Serbian magazines and newspapers. His short stories were included in the anthology *Shortest stories* (2006). He has co-authored the prose book *Diary 2000* (2001). His poetry collections are *Pressure* (2002), *Coping* (2006) and *Blessed Losers* (2009). His works have been translated into English, French, Polish and Catalan.

Mildred K. Barya is a writer and poet from Uganda. She was awarded the 2008 Pan African Literary Forum Prize for Africana Fiction, but had earlier gained recognition for her poetry, particularly her first two collections, *Men Love Chocolates but They don't Say* (2002) and *The Price of Memory: After the Tsunami* (2006). From August 2007 to August 2009, she served as Writer-In-Residence at Trust Africa, a Pan-African foundation based in Dakar, Senegal. She is a member of the Creative Writing Faculty at Alabama School of Fine Arts (ASFA).

Mimi Khalvati is an Iranian-born British poet. She has published eight collections of poetry with Carcanet Press, including *The Weather Wheel, The Meanest Flower*, a Poetry Book Society Recommendation, a Financial Times Book of the Year, and shortlisted for the TS Eliot Prize and, most recently, *Child: New and Selected Poems 1991-2011*, a Poetry Book Society Special Commendation. Her work has been translated into nine languages and she received Cholmondeley Award in 2006. She is a Fellow of the Royal Society of Literature. Mimi is the founder of The Poetry School and was its Coordinator from 1997–2004.

Moniza Alvi is a Pakistani-British poet and writer. *Peacock Luggage*, a book of poems by Moniza Alvi and Peter Daniels, was published as a result of the two poets jointly winning the Poetry Business Prize in 1991. Since then, Moniza Alvi has written eight poetry collections among which, *The Country at My Shoulder* (1993), was shortlisted for the T. S. Eliot Prize and the Whitbread Poetry Award, and which led to her being selected for

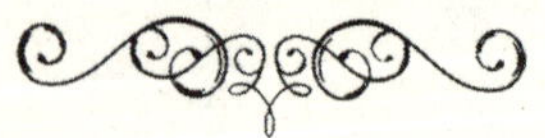

the Poetry Society's New Generation Poets promotion; *A Bowl of Warm Air* (1996), was one of the Independent on Sunday›s Books of the Year; *Carrying My Wife* (2000), a Poetry Book Society Recommendation; *and* Europa (2008), a Poetry Book Society Choice and was shortlisted for the TS Eliot prize.

Montserrat Villar González, graduate in Spanish and Portuguese Philology, has published three individual poetry books (*Tríptico de mármol*, Ed Huerga and Fierro; *Ternura incandescente*, Ed Huerga y Fierro; *La tierra con nosotros*, Ed Seleer), an author's book: *Desde la otra orilla* (together with five photographers). She has also been translated into Galician: *Terra de mármore e tenrura* (Anthology, Ed Lastura, translated by Xavier Frías Conde) and Portuguese: *Terra habitada* (Ed Palimage, translated by Jorge Fragoso). Besides, she has participated in numerous collective publications and magazines.

Morelle Smith is a poet, fiction and travel writer. She studied English and French Literature at Edinburgh University. She has been an adult education tutor (English, French & Creative Writing) for many years. Her work has been published in various print and online magazines and anthologies, including *Scottish Review, New Writing Scotland, Times Literary Supplement, The Salmon, The Dublin Quarterly, La Traductière, Ljubljana Tales* and *New Eastern Europe.* She has published several books of poetry and fiction, the most recent being– *Gold Tracks, Fallen Fruit* (Cestrian Press, 2011), and *Tirana Papers: An Albanian Journal* (Kairos, 2013).

Müesser Yeniay, poet and translator, was born in Izmir, Turkey in 1984. She has won several poetry prizes including Yunus Emre (2006), Homeros Attila İlhan (2007), Ali Riza Ertan (2009), and Enver Gökçe (2013) prize. Her first book *Dibine Düşüyor Karanlık da* was published in 2009 and her second book *Evimi Dağlara Kurdum* is a collection of translation from world poetry. Her latest book *Yeniden Çizdim Göğü* was published in 2011. Yeniay has also published a book on modern Turkish avant-garde poetry *The Other Consciousness: Surrealism and The*

Second New (2013). Yeniay is the poetry editor of the literary magazine *Şiirden*.

Myra Sklarew was educated at Tufts University and the Writing Seminars at Johns Hopkins University. She is the author of numerous poetry collections, most recently *Harmless* and *If You Want to Live Forever*. A new collection, *Sing, Little Collar Button*, is forthcoming, as is a research study, *A Survivor Named Trauma*. She taught literature at American University for nearly four decades where she founded and directed the MFA Program in Creative Writing. For the past three years she has worked on an archival project to document poets and poetry activities in the nation's capital from 1900 to the present.

Navid Haider studied Linguistics and Literature in English at North South University, Bangladesh. He has edited the annual existentialist school magazine, bluntly titled *English Matters* which chronicles the creative endeavours of first-year college students at his school. His work has been published in a short anthology called *Patchwork Pages*, sponsored by the American Culture Center and U.S. Embassy in Bangladesh in 2013.

Nguyen Bao Chan was born on November 23, 1969, at Haiphong in Vietnam. She graduated from the Writing and Editing Program of the Hanoi Cinema and Theater University in 1991, and currently works as an editor and scenarist for Vietnam Television. Nguyen Bao Chan has published two books: *The Burned River* (Dong Song Chay, 1994), which received an award from the Vietnamese Literary and Art Union and *Going Through Winter* (Chan tran qua vet ret), published in 1999. She is one of the one hundred Vietnamese poets included in the recent bilingual anthology The Defiant Muse: Vietnamese Poems from Antiquity to the Present, published in 2007.

Ngwatilo Mawiyoo, a native of Nairobi, Kenya, has steadily built a name for herself as a poet, performer, actress and musician. Ngwatilo's book of poems, *Blue Mothertongue* (2010), is set in

Nairobi addressing notions of home and identity of the African diaspora. Ngwatilo's work has been translated into Swedish and Austrian-German, in addition to being published in literary journals in Kenya and abroad. Ngwatilo has presented her work at major African and European festivals.

Nora Nadjarian is an award-winning poet and short story writer from Cyprus. She has published three collections of poetry: The Voice at the Top of the Stairs (2001), Cleft in Twain (2003) and 25 Ways to Kiss a Man (2004). Her work has won prizes and commendations in various international competitions: among others, in the Commonwealth Short Story Competition, the Féile Filíochta International Poetry Competition (Ireland) and the Binnacle International Ultra-Short Competition at the University of Maine at Machias, USA. Her work was included in Best European Fiction 2011 (Dalkey Archive Press) and in the poetry anthology *Being Human* (Bloodaxe Books, 2011).

Omar Sabbagh is a widely published poet and critic. Two of his extant collections are: *My Only Ever Oedipal Complaint* and *The Square Root of Beirut* (Cinnamon Press, 2010/12); a fourth collection: *To The Middle of Love* is forthcoming with Cinnamon. His Beirut novella, *Via Negativa: A Parable of Exile,* was published by Liquorice Fish Books in March 2016. A Dubai sequel to the latter, *From Bourbon to Scotch,* is forthcoming with Eyewear. He now teaches at the American University in Dubai (AUD).

Pascale Petit was born in Paris and lives in London. Her sixth collection *Fauverie* was shortlisted for the TS Eliot Prize and a portfolio of poems from it won the Manchester Poetry Prize. Her fifth book *What the Water Gave Me: Poems after Frida Kahlo* was shortlisted for both the TS Eliot Prize and Wales Book of the Year. She has published six collections, four of which were shortlisted for the TS Eliot Prize and three featured as Books of the Year in the *Times Literary Supplement*, *Observer* and *Independent*. She tutors for Tate Modern and The Poetry School.

Pat Boran, poet, writer and broadcaster is one of the best-known of his generation of Irish poets. He has published more than a dozen books of poetry and prose — among them his most recent poetry collection *The Next Life* (2012), the humorous memoir *The Invisible Prison (2009),* and the popular writers' handbook *The Portable Creative Writing Workshop,* recently reissued. He has also edited numerous anthologies of poetry and prose, including, with Gerard Smyth, the bestselling *If Ever You Go: A Map of Dublin in Poetry and Song, the Dublin: One City, One Book title for 2014.*

Pedro Pérez-Sarduy (1943) is an Afro-Cuban poet, writer, journalist, broadcaster and consultant on Cuba resident in London. He is the author of *Surrealidad* (Cuadernos UNION, Havana 1967); *Cumbite and Other Poems* – bilingual edition by Center for Cuban Studies, New York, 1990 and more recently, he published *Malecón Sigloveinte*, his latest poetry collection by Editorial Letras Cubanas, La Habana (2005). His poetry work can also found be in The Oxford Book of Caribbean Verse (2005). He is co-editor of *AFRO-CUBA: An Anthology of Cuban Writing on Race, Politics and Culture* (Ocean Press/Latin America Bureau, Melbourne/London, 1993) and co-author of *Introduction to No Longer Invisible/Afro-Latin Americans Today* (London 1995).

Philip McDonagh was born in Dublin in 1952 and attended schools in Dublin and Copenhagen, and University in Oxford. As a diplomat, he has had postings throughout Europe. Most recently he has been Irish Ambassador to India. In 1989, he was one of a group of five poets with introductory selections published as Dedalus Introductions and in 2003 published his first full-length collection with Dedalus, *Carraroe in Saxony*. Since then an expanded work, including this earlier book, has been published in India as *Memoirs of an Ionian Diplomat*. Philip McDonagh is currently Irish Ambassador to Russia.

Philip Nanton contributes articles, reviews and poetry to Anglophone literary magazines in the region including *Caribbean*

Review of Books, in Trinidad, *Poui, Bim and Arts Etc. in Barbados.* In 2012 he represented St. Vincent & the Grenadines at the Poetry Parnassus in London. In 2008 he launched his first spoken word CD and in 2014 he published an illustrated book version of the CD called *Island Voices from St Christopher & the Barracudas.* The collection was published by Papillote Press of London and Trafalgar, Dominica.

Philip Nikolayev, born in Moscow and raised in Russia and Moldova, is the son of a linguist. He grew up speaking both English and Russian and immigrated to the United States in 1990. Nikolayev earned a BA and an MA at Harvard University and a PhD at Boston University. His poetry collections include *Dusk Raga* (1998), *Monkey Time* (2003), which won a Verse prize, and *Letters from Aldenderry* (2006). Nikolayev is one of the founding editors of *Fulcrum* – an annual of poetry and aesthetics, and his work has been featured in *180 More Extraordinary Poems for Every Day* (2005).

Priya Sarukkai Chabria is a poet, novelist, essayist and translator with five published books. Awarded by the Indian Government for her Outstanding Contribution to Literature her works have been translated into six languages and is published in *Adelphiana*, *Asymptote*, *The Literary Review* (USA), South *Asian Review*, *Caravan*, *Cha*, *Post Road, The British Journal of Literary Translation, Drunken Boat* among others. Her books include translations of Tamil mystic poet Aandaal and a short story collection. She edits Poetry at Sangam (www.sangamhouse.org).

P.S. Cottier moved to Canberra in 1992, to take a job in the public service. The public service did not agree with her, but she has gradually discovered the poetry hidden in Canberra›s curves and mountains. She has published four books of poetry, the most recent being the anthology *The Stars Like Sand: Australian Speculative Poetry* (Interactive Publications 2014), which she edited with Tim Jones of New Zealand.

Reesom Haile was Eritrea's first internationally known poet. He wrote in Tigrinya, one of Eritrea's nine major languages. In exile during Eritrea's war for independence from Ethiopia, he served for over two decades as a Development Communications consultant, working with UN Agencies, governments and NGOs around the world before returning to Eritrea in 1994. His first collection of Tigrinya poetry, *Waza ms Qum Neger nTensae Hager* (1997), won the Raimok prize, Eritrea's highest award for literature. He published two other books of poetry, translated by Charles Cantalupo and published by Red Sea Press – *We Have Our Voice* (2000) and *We Invented the Wheel* (2002).

Rethabile Masilo is a Mosotho poet from Lesotho. His work has been published in various magazines, including Canopic Jar. Rethabile was born in 1961 in Lesotho and left his country with his parents and siblings to go into exile in 1981. In 2012 his first book of poems, Things That Are Silent, was published by Pindrop Press. The second book, Waslap, was published in 2015 by The Onslaught Press.

Reza Mohammadi is a prize-winning poet, widely regarded as one of the most exciting young poets writing in Persian today. He was born in Kandahar in 1979. His three collections of poetry have gained him many awards, including an award from the Afghan Ministry of Culture in 2004 and prizes for being Iran's best young poet in 1996 and 1997. Reza Mohammadi is also a prolific journalist and cultural commentator. He lives in London.

Russell Soaba was born in Tototo, Milne Bay in 1950. He was educated in Papua New Guinea, Australia and at Brown University, Providence, Rhode Island. Soaba is one of Papua New Guinea's most prolific writers. He currently teaches at the University of Papua New Guinea and works as an editor for a local publisher.

Ruth Padel is an award-winning British poet and writer, Poetry Fellow at King's College London, Fellow of the Royal Society of Literature and Council Member for the Zoological Society of

London. Her tenth poetry collection, *Learning to Make an Oud in Nazareth* was shortlisted for the 2014 T. S. Eliot Prize. She has also published a novel on wildlife crime, *Where the Serpent Lives*, and eight books of non-fiction including *I'm A Man: Sex, Gods and Rock 'n' Roll* which weaves together Greek myth rock music and opera, and *Tigers in Red Weather* on wild tiger conservation. She teaches poetry at King's College, London, is Ambassador for *New Networks for Nature*, and patron of *21st Century Tiger*.

Sabrina Masud is from Dhaka, Bangladesh. She wrote this poem on Tbilisi, capital of Georgia after she saw a photograph of a Georgian woman. She could picture the whole city in this woman's distant eyes and her tilted chin, the proud slant of her eye brows. Sabrina likes to sketch, but the shadows on this woman's face were too much for her pencils, so she decided to use words.

Salah Al Hamdani was born in Baghdad. He's the author of some thirty books in both Arabic and French. At age seventeen he was incarcerated for opposing the dictatorship. Too poor to have attended school, other political prisoners taught him how to read and write. He composed his first poems in prison.

Saradha Soobrayen was born in London and received a Society of Authors Eric Gregory Award in 2004 and was named in the Guardian newspaper as one of the 'Twelve to watch', up and coming new generation of poets. She represented the island of Mauritius at the Southbank Centre's Parnassus Poetry festival in 2013 and was awarded the Pacuare Nature Reserve's Poet Laureate residency in Costa Rica in 2015-16. Saradha's critical texts, experimental short fiction and poetry are widely published in journals and anthologies.

Scott Alain draws his inspiration from the sounds and citizens of downtown Ottawa. Growing up in the city, he tries to capture its atmosphere and the essence of its inhabitants in his work. He is a supplementary instruction facilitator and student of anthropology at Carleton University. As an emerging writer, he has recently

begun to enjoy publication in multiple local and national poetry collections.

Sharanya Manivannan's first book of poems, *Witchcraft*, was described in *The Straits Times* as 'sensuous and spiritual, delicate and dangerous and as full as the moon reflected in a knife'. Her forthcoming books include *The Ammuchi Puchi*, *The High Priestess Never Marries* and *The Altar of the Only World*. Sharanya writes a personal column, *The Venus Flytrap*, for *The New Indian Express*. Her fiction, poetry and essays have been widely published internationally, and she was specially commissioned to write and perform a poem at the 2015 Commonwealth Day Observance in London. She lives in India.

Shurooq Amin (b.1967) is a Kuwaiti mixed-media interdisciplinary artist and an Anglophone poet. Her poetry has been published into two books, in more than 40 literary journals, and has been anthologized in the *Gathering the Tide: An Anthology of Arabian Gulf Poetry* by Ithaca Publishers in association with the Virginia Commonwealth University of Qatar. Her second volume of poetry "*The Hanging of the Wind*" is taught as part of contemporary literature curriculum in universities in the Gulf. She is the first Kuwaiti to be nominated for the prestigious Pushcart Prize in December 2007.

Sitawa Namwalie is a Kenyan poet, writer and performer. She is a lyrical storyteller who deals with the complex issue of Kenyan identity. From her reflections on ethnicity, identity, land ownership, dominion and love she created *Cut Off My Tongue* – a poetry collection published by Storymoja and was invited to Hay Festival (UK 2009). Sitawa is working on her second poetry anthology and has a new performance called *Silence is a Woman*.

Steven J. Fowler is a contemporary British poet and an avant-garde artist. He works in the modernist and avant-garde traditions, across poetry, fiction, sonic art, visual art, installation and performance. He has published six collections of poetry and was

commissioned by the Tate, Highlight Arts, Mercy, Penned in the Margins and the London Sinfonietta. He has been translated into 13 languages and performed at venues across the world, from Mexico City to Erbil, Iraq. He is the poetry editor of 3am magazine and is the curator of the Enemies project.

Sudeep Sen's prize-winning books include *Postmarked India: New & Selected Poems* (HarperCollins), *Rain, Aria* (A. K. Ramanujan Translation Award), *The HarperCollins Book of English Poetry* (editor), *Fractals: New & Selected Poems | Translations 1980-2015* (London Magazine Editions) and *EroText* (Vintage: Penguin Random House). *Blue Nude: New Poems & Ekphrasis* (Jorge Zalamea International Poetry Prize) is forthcoming. Sen's works have been translated into over 25 languages. Sen's newer work appears in *New Writing 15* (Granta), *Language for a New Century* (Norton), *Leela: An Erotic Play of Verse and Art* (Collins), *Indian Love Poems* (Knopf/Random House/Everyman), *Out of Bounds* (Bloodaxe), and *Initiate: Oxford New Writing* (Blackwell).

Sudesh Mishra, poet, playwright, short fiction writer and academic, was born in 1962 in Suva to an Indo-Fijian family and educated in Fiji and Australia. His work has been published in several anthologies, including The Bloodaxe Book of Contemporary Indian Poetry, Lines Review: Twelve Modern Young Indian Poets, Concert of Voices: An Anthology of World Writing in English, Nuanua: Pacific Writing in English since 1980, among others. He is Professor in Literature and Linguistics at the University of the South Pacific. He is the author of four books of poems and is currently at work on his fifth.

Tabish Khair (b. 1966) and educated in India, is the author of a number of books, including studies, poetry collections and novels. Winner of the All India Poetry Prize and fellowships at Hong Kong, Delhi and Cambridge, Khair's novels have been shortlisted for the Encore Award (UK), Vodafone Crossword Award (India), Hindu Best Fiction Prize (India), Man Asian Literature Prize

(Hong Kong/UK), DSC Prize for South Asia (UK/India), Aloa Prize (Denmark) etc. His new novel, *How to Fight Islamist Terror from the Missionary Position*, was dubbed 'unmissable' by the Times and 'irreverent, intelligent, explosive' by the Independent. Back in 1997, he moved to Copenhagen to do a PhD and has, since then, settled down in a village off Aarhus, Denmark retaining his Indian passport.

Tanja Bakic is a Montenegrin poet, literary scholar and translator. She graduated with an MA in English Language and Literature from University of Montenegro. She is the author of five imagistic poetry collections, the first of which was published when she was fifteen years old. Her poetry has received numerous accolades, and has been translated into ten languages and presented across Europe. She has contributed an aural component to a plant installation by Australian eco-designer, Tanja Beer, presented by Arts House (Melbourne) in partnership with Cambridge Junction, UK. She is responsible for the Montenegrin component of the world poetry festival 'Palabra en el Mundo'.

Temirkhan Medetbek was born 1945 in the town of Turkestan, South Kazakhstan. First published in 1970 he has published more than ten books of poetry. In 2000 he was awarded The State Prize of the Republic of Kazakhstan. *The spirit of Blue Turks* is one of his significant poetry collections.

Tim Cummings was born in Solihull and brought up in the West Country. His poetry collections include *The Miniature Estate (1991), Apocalypso (1992, 1999), Contact Print (2002) and The Rumour (2004).* His poems have appeared in magazines including Magma, Poetry London, The London Magazine, Boomerang and Limelight. His work has appeared in numerous anthologies, including the Bloodaxe Books' major 2010 anthology of poetry from Ireland and the British Isles, Identity Parade.

Todd Swift was born in Montreal, on Good Friday, 1966, and grew up in St-Lambert, Quebec. Swift is included in the

Oxford Companion to Modern Poetry in English (2013). He has published 9 full poetry collections, many more pamphlets, and edited or co-edited numerous international anthologies. He holds a PhD in creative and critical writing from the UEA. He is Director of Eyewear Publishing.

Tomica Bajsic was born in 1968 in Zagreb, Croatia. A poet, prose writer, graphic designer and translator he edited and translated poetry for Poezija/Poetry quarterly magazine, Croatia, and is the founder and the chief editor at Druga priča /Another Story publishing. He worked as the General Secretary of Croatian PEN Centre. His poetry and prose pieces have been translated into twelve languages. He is the author of six books of poetry and prose, and a picture book.

Tony Tcheka (António Soares Lopes Júnior, born in Bissau, 1951) was one of the founders of the National Artists and Writers Union, Guinea-Bissau. He is considered a reference in Guinean literature, with works published in various anthologies in Guinea-Bissau, Portugal, France, Brazil and Germany.

Valzhyna Mort, born in Minsk, Belarus, in 1981, has been praised as '[a] risen star of the international poetry world' by the *Irish Times*. Her first book of poetry, *I'm as Thin as Your Eyelashes*, came out in Belarus in 2005. In 2004 in Slovenia she received a Crystal Vilencia Award for best poetry performance. She was the recipient, in 2005, of a Gaude Polonia scholarship in Poland, and, in 2006, of a writing fellowship from Literarisches Colloquium Berlin, Germany. Her first American publication, *Factory of Tears* (Copper Canyon Press, 2008), the first Belarusian/English poetry book published in the U.S., was co-translated from the Belarusian by Elizabeth Oehlkers Wright and Pulitzer Prize-winning poet Franz Wright.

Veronica Zondek was born in Santiago de Chile in 1953. She is a poet, translator and cultural manager. With a BA in Art History at the Hebrew University of Jerusalem, she is part of the editorial

board of LOM Ediciones and magazines in Chile and abroad. She has served on the jury of competitions such as the Council of Books, Fondart, Chilectra and Santibán and has twice received the scholarship granted by the Fund Book for writing, in 1997 and 2006. Her poems and articles have appeared in journals of national and foreign literature.

Vladimir Lucien was born in St. Lucia on in 1988. While attending St. Mary's College (1999-2004) Lucien stumbled upon his 'first art': acting, starring in a number of plays produced by the school's drama club. After leaving school, Lucien took up a teaching job, which he resigned from after a year to pursue acting in New York. When this proved discouraging, Lucien returned to St. Lucia shortly in 2008, and subsequently took up studies at the University of the West Indies in Trinidad where he began writing poetry seriously. In October 2011 he graduated with honors from the University with a degree in Literatures in English and Theatre Arts.

Victoria Guerrero Peirano is a poet, teacher and researcher. She has a PhD in Hispanic Literature from Boston University and has published several books of poems, including *El mar ese oscuro porvenir* (2002), *Ya nadie incendia el mundo* (2005) and more recently *Berlin* (2011). She has taken part in poetry festivals in cities like Berlin, Boston, Providence, Buenos Aires, Quito, Santiago and Lima, and is the editor of Intermezzo Tropical, a magazine specialising in literature and politics. She is a professor at Pontificia Universidad Católica del Perú in Lima.

Vijay Seshadri was born in Bangalore, India, in 1954 and came to America at the age of five. His collections of poems include James Laughlin Award winner *The Long Meadow* (Graywolf Press, 2004) and *Wild Kingdom* (1996). His poems, essays, and reviews have appeared in *AGNI, the American Scholar, the Nation, the New Yorker, the Paris Review, Shenandoah, Southwest Review, Threepenny Review, Verse, Yale Review, the Times Book Review, among others*, and in many anthologies. Seshadri is the author of *Wild Kingdom* (1996); *The Long Meadow* (2003), which won the

James Laughlin Award; and *3 Sections* (2013), which won the Pulitzer Prize in Poetry.

Viola Allo is a Cameroonian-born poet based in the United States. Her poems and essays have been published in the American River Review. In 2011, her poem "Nigerian Girl with Calabash" was published in US Poet Laureate Kay Ryan's community college poetry anthology, *Poetry for the Mind's Joy*. In 2011, the poem was selected as "Best in the Nation" by the Community College Humanities Association. Viola was shortlisted for the Brunel University African Poetry Prize in 2013 and again in 2014.

Willem M. Roggeman, a Flemish poet born in Brussels was called 'a painter with words'. It is indeed painting which has had the most influence on his poetry. Roggeman was for a long time a professional journalist and art critic. He is writing poetry, novels, plays and essays.

Xavier Frias Conde is a Spanish writer born in 1965. He currently works as a lecturer at the Spanish UNED (Distance University), where he teaches linguistics. As a writer, he has published a dozen books in several languages, mainly Galician-Portuguese and Spanish. He also writes children's literature. He is an active blogger, a translator and even a publisher. He belongs to the so-called Grupo Bilbao of Galician writers living in Madrid, being one of its founders, and belongs to Aveiro Poetry Group in Portugal.

Yeşim Ağaoğlu, born January 21, 1966 in Istanbul, Turkey, is a multidisciplinary artist and a poet who works with various media, especially concentrating on installation, photography and video. Her family comes from the city of Shusha in the Karabagh region of Azerbaijan. The most important thing for her in art is being interactive. She works on poetry (language) and art relationships, gender and feminism issues, architectural elements and political subjects. Since 1995 Agaoglu has produced nine poetry books that have made her famous as a women poet in the literature scene of Turkey.

Yusuf M. Adamu is a Professor of Medical Geography at the Bayero University Kano, Nigeria. His literary works include *Idan So Cuta ne* and *Maza Gumbar Dutse* (Hausa novels), *Landscapes of Reality, They Can Speak English* and *A Flat World* (poetry), *Clever Squirrel and the Great Wedding Contest.*

Zaharaddeen Ibrahim Kallah holds a BSc. Sociology/Political Science, and Masters in Development Studies. He is a bilingual writer, writing in English and Hausa languages. He works with the Directorate of Academic Planning, Bayero University, Kano. Zaharaddeen is an-award winning writer. His significant works are: *Sadauki Mai Duniya,* and a collection of poems entitled, *After a Long Silence*.

Zoë Brigley was born in 1981 and grew up in Caerphilly in the Rhymney Valley. She won an Eric Gregory Award in 2003 and received an Academy bursary in 2005. Her first book of poems, *The Secret* (Bloodaxe Books, 2007), was a Poetry Book Society Recommendation, and was long listed for the Dylan Thomas Prize in 2008. Her second collection, *Conquest* (Bloodaxe Books, 2012), was also a Poetry Book Society Recommendation. She has taught creative writing at Warwick University and at University of Northampton.

POETS INDEX

CAPITALS INDEX